Library of
Davidson College

body movement
PERSPECTIVES IN RESEARCH

body movement
PERSPECTIVES IN RESEARCH

Advisory Editor: Martha Davis
Hunter College

TOWARDS UNDERSTANDING THE INTRINSIC IN BODY MOVEMENT

Martha Davis

ARNO PRESS
A NEW YORK TIMES COMPANY
New York • 1975

Reprint Edition 1975 by Arno Press Inc.

Copyright © 1973 by Martha Davis

Reprinted by permission of Dr. Martha Davis

Body Movement: Perspectives in Research
ISBN for complete set: 0-405-06197-8
See last pages of this volume for titles.

Manufactured in the United States of America

Library of Congress Cataloging in Publication Data

Davis, Martha.
    Towards understanding the intrinsic in body movement.

    (Body movement: perspectives in research)
    Originally presented as the author's thesis, Yeshiva University, 1973.
    Bibliography: p.
    1. Movement, Psychology of. 2. Expression. I. Title. II. Series.
BF295.D38   1974   152.3   74-7857
ISBN 0-405-06200-1

TABLE OF CONTENTS

I. Introduction	7
II. Literature Review	10
Emotion	12
Personality and Psychopathology	14
Psychological Interpretation of Specific Actions	17
Interaction and Communication	19
Cultural Comparisons	22
Developmental Patterns	24
Concluding Remarks	26
III. Drawing on Movement Notation Systems for a Glossary of Movement Terms	29
A Survey of Three Notation Systems	29
Labanotation	31
Eshkol-Wachmann Movement Notation	32
Effort-Shape Analysis	33
Development of a Movement Glossary	34
Movement Glossary	37
IV. Application of the Movement Glossary to the Literature	45
V. Correlations Between Specific Movement Patterns and Behavioral Phenomena	67
Consistencies in Parameter Selection	67
Analysis of Movement Style	69
VI. The Question of Intrinsic Significance	75
Three Types of Relationships Between Movement and Its Significance	76
Arbitrary vs. Iconic or Intrinsic	80
Literature Evidence	80
Different Types of Correlations	84
Iconic vs. Intrinsic	89
Parsimony	90
Isomorphism	90

    Central Organizing Principles 93
    Concluding Remarks 93

VII. Theoretical Considerations and Implications for
  Future Research 96
    *Theoretical Model for Integrating Diverse
    Areas of Movement Research* 97
    A Possible Future Direction for Movement Research ... 102
    Concluding Remarks 105

Bibliography 109

Appendices:

 I. Descriptions of the Seventeen References Used
  For Glossary Analysis 117
 II. Selected References on Movement Notation Systems
  And Their Application 129

LIST OF TABLES

Table 1. Historical Perspective of Movement Research 27

Table 2. Three Analyses of the Same Movement 35

Table 3. Works Considered for Glossary Analysis 48

Table 4. Movement Analysis of Literature Examples 54

Table 5. Movement Parameters Used to Differentiate
   Different Levels of Analysis 71

LIST OF FIGURES

Figure 1. Theoretical Correlations Between Movement
    Parameters and Specific Behavioral Phenomena 98

ACKNOWLEDGEMENTS

This book was originally a doctoral thesis submitted to the Ferkauf Graduate School of Humanities, Yeshiva University, New York City. A theoretical dissertation seems to be something of an anomaly in psychology and I want to thank those whose help and willingness to gamble enabled me to do it: my chairman, Dr. Carl Auerbach, and committee members, Drs. Norman Gordon and Gilbert Voyat. My thanks also to Dr. Adam Kendon for his advice on the first chapters and to Dr. Paul Byers for his vote of confidence at a time when it was most appreciated. I particularly appreciate the contribution of my students at Hunter College; our discussions helped clarify and sharpen my thinking on movement research.

This thesis is the culmination of over eight years of work, so it seems appropriate to take this opportunity to thank some people who have been very important to me over these years. I want to thank Dr. Israel Zwerling who first acknowledged the potential of our work and supported it at Albert Einstein. My deep appreciation to Irmgard Bartenieff with whom I first apprenticed and whose vision has always been a source of wonder to me.

The ways that my parents, Harry and Mary Davis, contributed to my learning are immeasurable and I thank them especially. It is difficult to express thanks to my husband, Sergio Rothstein—words for this seem trite and detached and his support and care has been anything but pro forma.

Finally, I would like to dedicate this work to George Kaufer whose friendship and help has been so precious.

Chapter I

INTRODUCTION

One is in motion all the time. Nearly every human activity—talking, walking, working, etc.—involves a complex medley of breathing patterns, eye movements, postures, limb actions, facial expressions, orientations in space. Although all of movement can be described in kinesiological or neurophysiological terms, any movement behavior, whether it is walking down a street, scratching one's nose, or sitting in a living room, also has psychological and sociological aspects.

In 1970 and '71 this author prepared an annotated bibliography of the literature on the psychology and anthropology of body movement (variously called nonverbal communication, kinesics, expressive movement, body language). The list of people who have given serious attention to body movement reads like a Who's Who in the behavioral sciences, although much of this work is isolated and obscure. Darwin's treatise on the expression of emotions established body motion as a subject of serious scientific interest 100 years ago, but there have been only two periods of intensive, collective research on the subject, one in the 1920's and '30's and one now. It is clear that a renaissance in the behavioral study of body movement is occurring; indeed over the past ten years there has been virtually a geometric increase in such research.

The importance of the study of movement to psychology and anthropology is beginning to be widely recognized. Careful analysis of films and videotapes has revealed that movement and postural behavior is critical in the maintenance and regulation of face-to-face interaction (cf. Scheflen, 1965). Naturalistic observation of infants and children indicates that movement patterns may be related to cognitive as well as personality development (Kestenberg et al., 1972). There is evidence that one can diagnose schizophrenic symptoms from body movement patterns (Wolff, 1945; Davis, 1970). Analyses of the psychological significance of various gestures or actions performed by a patient in psychotherapy suggests that movements can be immediate and visible reflections of attitudes and feelings that are out of conscious awareness (Mahl, 1968; Deutsch, 1952).

A review of literature on the subject, such as will be presented in the next chapter, shows that there is a great diversity of approach and very little synthesis of results or methods. Of course, the range of disciplines covered when one surveys movement research per se is broad, from anthropology to physiological psychology, and an anthropologist will use different terms and methods than an experimental psychologist. Because each study reflects the terminology, methods, and focus of the researcher's discipline, it often results that concepts and methods originally developed for the study of verbal behavior, perception, or cognitive processes are applied to movement, a dimension that has its own unique properties. Although there are inevitably differences in goals and methods between researchers who investigate movement in the framework of their different disciplines, there is also a place for comparison of approaches and results.

If one were to stand back and survey the research on body movement, it would look at first like a mass of isolated and often contradictory observations. However, if one uses a particular "prism" or "lens" for this scanning, much of the literature forms a coherent pattern and it is possible to see more interrelationships between research results than contradictions. It is an assumption of the current work that one "prism" that makes this possible is the perspective provided by movement analysis systems. What is striking about most behavioral research on body movement is the lack of a systematic language for describing movement in its own terms. It will be shown that much of the ambiguity and contradiction in movement research is removed when it is made clear what aspects of movement are being assessed, with what terminology, and in what degree of detail. One of the practical tasks of this thesis will be to show how movement notation systems originally developed for recording dance are useful in providing a language for behavioral studies, as well as being logical, comprehensive ways for analyzing movement. It is further assumed here that embedded within these systems are concepts and principles of analysis that have value for interpretation as well as for systematic description.

The thesis will evolve in the following way. First, principal trends in behavioral research on body movement will be presented. Next, a summary of major movement notation systems—i.e., systems for recording movement (Labanotation, Effort-Shape Analysis, and Eshkol-Wachmann movement notation)—will be presented and a list of movement terms that should be relevant to behavioral research will be abstracted from them. The fourth chapter, using this framework, examines the literature surveyed in Chapter II with respect to which aspects of movement are studied and in what detail. The next chapter shows that particular movement parameters are typically used in the study of psychological and cultural phenomena—e.g., assessments of chronic muscle tension patterns are frequently correlated with psychological defenses, while analyses of seating arrangements are correlated with social role relationships.

The next chapter examines why this is so. It will be shown that not only are there consistent relationships between specific movement parameters and specific behavioral phenomena, but that there are also consistencies in how movement patterns are interpreted. It is hypothesized that such consistencies in interpretation reflect what will be called "intrinsic", or fundamental, relationships between the movement and its significance(s) and that resemblances between the movement and what it is associated with are not arbitrary. The dissertation concludes with proposals of a model which integrates the research reviewed and a new line of research which is suggested by the analysis.

In summary, the thesis progresses from a traditional review of the literature to a systematic reassessment of it, using movement analysis concepts as a clarifying "prism." Pursuing the idea that much of the literature can be clarified and integrated when one focuses on the movement dimension and its nature and particular properties, the thesis is extended to an analysis of what parameters of movement are commonly associated with what behavioral phenomena and why. In this way a number of controversies will be shown to be empty. A final chapter will discuss the implications of this analysis for future research.

Of necessity this is a work-in-progress. The field of movement research is growing too fast, is far too complex, and requires a much greater input from such disciplines as anthropology and psychology for this to be anything more than an initial step toward the synthesis of diverse approaches. But while conclusive statements would be absurd at this point, a systematic overview would seem of value in clarifying issues, defining trends, and articulating new hypotheses.

Chapter II

LITERATURE REVIEW

   Modern scientific study of movement behavior began in 1872 with the publication of Darwin's *The Expression of the Emotions in Man and Animals,* an unparalleled treatise on the origins and functions of facial and bodily expressions. Darwin observed the movements of those around him, himself, and his animals. He enlisted the help of missionaries and British colonists to inform him about patterns of body expression in various cultures. Their replies to his questionnaire showed, for example, that like Europeans, Indians shrug their shoulders to express helplessness, but unlike Europeans, Turks nod their heads in negation not affirmation (Darwin, 1965 ed., p. 274). He solicited information from doctors at a London asylum on the facial expressions and body movements of mental patients and accumulated evidence that certain movements correlate with certain mental conditions. He also had people judge the emotions expressed in a series of photographs and found that there was considerable agreement for certain expressions.

   Darwin regarded the behaviors he observed, from the prance of his dog to the frown of a person in deep thought, as subject to the same laws of natural selection, adaptation, modification, and extinction as are bodily structures (Darwin, 1965 ed., p. xii). He was, in effect, a naturalist of body expression; he observed a wide range of animal and human behaviors in their natural contexts and compared, contrasted, and assessed them with an accurate eye in a determined search for clues to their adaptive functions. Out of 30-odd years of such observations, he formulated theories of the origins and functions of these behaviors.

Primary among these theories is the principle of "serviceable associated habits": that certain acts are performed to relieve certain states or sensations and that when the state recurs the action may recur through a process of habit and association, even though it may no longer be adaptive (Darwin, 1965 ed., p. 28). Under this principle Darwin includes a wide variety of acts, including the startle reflex, angry facial expression, and scratching the head when perplexed. Within Darwin's framework an act or facial expression may be the evolutionary vestige of a very old behavior such as when a domesticated dog circles the carpet like his wild ancestors did to flatten the grass before bedding down (Darwin, 1965 ed., p. 43). Whatever the body expression, Darwin asked why it had that form, what purpose it served, what action pattern could it be derived from.

Darwin presents copious examples in support of his three main principles: (1) the principle of serviceable associated habits, which has already been discussed; (2) the principle of antithesis, which holds that while a given state of mind might lead to a given adaptive movement, the opposite state might lead to a movement opposite to the first but having no clear function. For example, a dog poised erect and rigid in a dangerous situation is in an adaptive position, but the function of the opposite attitude of crouching down, tail wagging, and ears depressed in "joy" at seeing his owner is not clear. It seems to be the antithesis of the first; the opposite state producing the opposite movement; and (3) the principle of direct action of the nervous system—i.e., a certain movement, such as trembling, may result from excessive excitation of the nervous system.

Darwin's work appears to have stimulated the wealth of facial-recognition studies done by German and American psychologists in the 1920's and 1930's. His observations of animal displays were not followed up until the growth of ethology in the 1950's, and cultural comparisons of the order he envisioned are only now being attempted. Little wonder that ethologists, psychologists, and anthropologists may each claim Darwin for their own, and recent editions of his book can be as enthusiastically prefaced by Margaret Mead as by Konrad Lorenz.

After Darwin the "field" of body movement research fragmented according to traditional behavioral disciplines. Most of the behavioral literature on movement can be divided into six categories; topics of research that evolved independently until the "movement movement" of the 1960's and '70's (Davis, 1972). Roughly speaking, these divisions are movement in relation to:

    Emotion
    Personality and Psychopathology

    Psychological Interpretation of Specific Actions
    Interaction and Communication
    Cultural Comparisons
    Developmental Patterns

The following literature review will trace each topic over time, concentrating on works considered of key importance within each division (see Table 1). The reader is referred to Appendix I for more extensive descriptions of certain of these important works.

EMOTION

The literature on movement and emotion falls into two main areas: facial-recognition studies and behavioral studies of muscle tension.

In the 1920's and 1930's, as has been mentioned, there was a great deal of research by American and European psychologists on the recognition of facial expression (cf. Frois-Wittman, 1930; Landis, 1929; Ruckmick, 1921; Jenness, 1932; Goodenough, 1931; Kanner, 1931; Jarden and Fernberger, 1926). In a search for reliable, overt manifestations of emotions, these studies typically involved having people judge the expressions in various photos. For example, Frois-Wittman (1930) presented photos of posed subjects to 165 judges and asked them to check which emotions from a list of 43 terms best described the facial expressions. High agreement was found on some terms. As it developed, however, the results of facial-recognition studies appeared mixed. For example, Landis (1929) found that observers judged the emotions with no better than chance accuracy, whereas Goodenough (1931) found that the judges were correct in over 45% of the matchings. These studies were originally considered as investigations into the nature of emotion; presumably, if facial expressions could be reliably identified, this would support the theory that there are primary emotions that are universally displayed and understood. While the recognition studies markedly decreased after 1940, a few modern studies have continued the thread of this work; these largely support Darwin's initial hypotheses but develop them further. For example, Frijda has presented experimental evidence that judgments differ both according to features of the facial expression and according to situational cues. Facial expressions are found to reflect a "general aspect of the person's emotional state," while the situational cues give the interpretation specificity (Frijda, 1953, 1958). Schlosberg (1954) conducted recognition studies showing that facial expressions (and perhaps by extension, emotions) factored along three dimensions: attention-rejection, pleasant-unpleasant, and sleep-tension. Research in facial expression has evolved considerably since 1910 to include empirical studies of when and how expressions actually occur, how they develop, the influence of the situation on their interpretation, and their function as social cues or communication signals. The most notable current work in this tradition is that of Ekman and Friesen on pan-cultural recognition of facial expression. They have found that members of very different cultures interpreted certain facial expressions similarly (Ekman, Sorenson and Friesen, 1969). They have also developed a "facial affect scoring technique" that successfully predicts observers' judgments of facial expression (Ekman, Friesen and Tomkins, 1971). While there are scattered studies of the recognition of affect from body posture or hand gestures, such studies are surprisingly rare—perhaps in part reflecting what appears to be a widespread assumption, articulated by Tomkins (1962), that the face is "the primary site of the affects."

Throughout the theoretical literature on the nature of emotions there are references to the role of movements and muscle tension patterns in affective processes (Lange and James, 1922; Plutchik, 1954), most elaborately presented by Nina Bull (1951), citing research in which specific postures were induced in response to specific emotion terms during hypnosis. Muscle tension in relation to emotions and anxiety has been the subject of considerable research since the 1930's (Barlow, 1955; Braatoy, 1952; R. C. Davis, 1942; Loraas, 1960; Plutchik, 1954). Alexander Luria (1932) conducted elaborate muscle tension studies of people under severe stress—students before important exams, suspects on trial, etc.—and traced patterns of disorganization under stress in kymographic recordings. Jacobsen (1967) conducted over 35 years of research on the relation between muscle activity, as measured by the EMG, and emotion, severe anxiety, thinking, and perception. The magnitude and patterning of muscle activity (whether measured mechanically, electrically, or through observation) have long been correlated with excitation and anxiety. While a simple correlation is often made between anxiety and increased muscle tension, sophisticated analyses report more subtle possibilities such as between muscle activity and empathy, attention, and personality characteristics. For example, Malmo et al. have found relationships between increased tension and irregular patterns of muscle activity and psychopathology (1951). Some of their extensive research has produced very specific data such as that increased tension in the arm muscles may be associated with hostility topics while leg tension was found associated with sex themes (Malmo et al., 1956). Recent work by Clynes (1970) suggests that there may be specific muscle activity waves for specific emotions, and Kestenberg (1965b) correlates specific "tension flow curves" with particular psychosexual drives. Hunt (1970) has reported preliminary indications that it may be possible to determine from muscle activity patterns whether the movements arise from the spinal level, the brain stem, or the cortex at any given time. The neurophysiological emphasis of most research on muscle tension and affect is apparent, but a few recent studies focus on interpersonal aspects of muscle activity patterns. For example, Malmo et al. (1957) have found certain uniformities in the muscle activities of both patient and examiner while the patient was being criticized. Muscle tension research appears to be particularly important in the study of conflict and anxiety; recent research indicates that sophisticated analysis may make possible the study of specific emotions.

PERSONALITY AND PSYCHOPATHOLOGY

Darwin found that certain mental disorders were characterized by specific fixed expressions and early works on psychiatric nosology included movement disturbances as important diagnostic criteria (cf. Bleuler, 1950 ed.). Ferenczi (1921) wrote on the psychoanalysis of tics and Breuer and Freud (1895) analyzed the psychological significance of various muscle contractions and movements in relation to hysterical neuroses. Charlotte Wolff (1945) reports research on the movement characteristics of hospitalized mental patients, as does Davis (1970). And Lowen (1967) has analyzed disturbances in body image, movement, and posture in the schizoid personality in his book *The Betrayal of the Body*. While these works are comprehensive and full of implications as to the relationships between motor disturbances and psychiatric disorders, they remain relatively isolated examples. In recent years researchers have made observations about disturbances in the timing, organization, and duration of the body movements of schizophrenic patients (cf. Birdwhistell, 1970, p. 24; Condon, 1968), but these observations are rather rare in the body of their works.

The more general question as to whether and in what way movement patterns may be related to personality has also been relatively little researched, although common sense suggests that one's movement style is a clue to one's character. Again, major studies in this area are rare but comprehensive. Allport and Vernon (1933) attempted to experimentally assess the consistency of individual movement patterns, on the assumption that the measurement of overt expression was the most direct way to study personality. They had 25 men perform a wide range of motor tasks. Various measures of speed, pressure, muscle tension, co-ordination, and spatial patterns were obtained from psychophysical tests and observation. Allport and Vernon were essentially taking the first step in an empirical study of movement and personality, providing data on the question of whether an individual's movement patterns are in fact consistent across time and task. They also present clinical data that indicate that the expressive movement styles of their subjects are compatible with independent personality descriptions of them. Allport and Vernon also found that three movement factors could be derived from the tests: an "areal," or expansive, factor; an emphasis factor; and a centrifugal, or "outward tendency," factor. However, the relationships between the motor factors and personality traits were clearly not simple ones. While there are a number of psychomotor tests of personality (Takala, 1953), experimental study of expressive manner in relation to personality seems largely confined to the work of Allport and Vernon.

There is a curious phenomenon in behavioral research on movement. Before the 1960's there were a few isolated "classics," works written with vision and depth yet, in spite of their promise, virtually ignored as inspirations for further research. Darwin's is such a classic, as is Allport and Vernon's book. Efron wrote one in anthropology (1941), and Krout conducted original studies on the psychological interpretation of gesture in the 1930's. Typically these works remained obscure through the years when their subjects were of little interest and then became sources of surprise and note when interest in body movement recurred. They are still relevant and timely—a fact that makes them appropriate for analysis in this thesis despite their age.

The next work to be discussed is another such singular classic, Wilhelm Reich's *Character Analysis,* a study of the relationships between muscle tension, posture, bodily expression, and character (Reich, 1949). Unlike Allport and Vernon's book, this work is theoretical, clinical, and psychoanalytic. It is also a seminal work on the psychological interpretation of breathing, postures, and movement patterns, one whose influence can be seen in the new psychotherapies (cf. Perls, Hefferline, and Goodman, 1951). Like Darwin, Reich articulates certain theories about expressive movement that are now so widely taken for granted they are not always assumed to have an author.

And like Darwin's, Reich's work on the body was a logical outgrowth of his general line of investigation. In Reich's case it followed naturally that if an analyst was to shift his attention from isolated psychological symptoms to a general character analysis, then he must attend to the patient's expressive style and overt manner, the way he walks, sits, talks, gestures, holds himself, etc. He noted that concentration on verbal content alone often obstructed the therapy and he considered the patient's mode of behavior to be at least as important as what he said, dreamed, or did, and perhaps more important in revealing affect.

> It is to be noted that the analysis of the "what"—in spite of the unity of content and form—leaves the "how" untouched; that this "how" turns out to be the hiding-place of the same psychic contents which already seem to be dissolved or made conscious by the analysis of the "what"; and finally, that the analysis of the "how" is particularly effective in releasing the affects. (Reich, 1949, p. 188)

Reich assumed that personality characteristics and a psychological mechanism such as repression must be established in the soma as well as in the psyche. While he might have rested with pointing out the value of movements simply as clues to character, as "epiphenomena" useful in diagnosis, he took his observations more seriously. He evolved theories that regarded body expression, breathing, and muscle tension patterns as one with psychic processes critical in personality development and as essential aspects of psychological defenses.

At times Reich's analysis of what he calls "character armor" is literally an assessment of "muscle armoring"—chronic tensions and specific fixed expressions of the face or body. From his descriptions of specific character neuroses, one can cull out what Reich regarded as movement patterns typical of each. For example, he notes that chronic hypertonia, rigidity of expression, and a certain unrhythmical, awkward manner are typical of the compulsive character, while the hysterical character often exhibits soft, agile, sinuous movements with an element of nervous evasion and sexual provocativeness. Reich goes beyond character typing to an analysis of the origins and functions of various breathing and muscle patterns. He posits, for example, that specific tensions in various parts of the body function as defenses against the experience and discharge of affect—e.g., a chronic attitude of holding back (shoulders pulled back, chin rigid, respiration shallow, lower back arched) reflects a chronic defense against rage and aggression. He posits that there is a segmental arrangement of the muscle armor: seven "rings" of tension—for example, the "oral ring" of tension around the mouth, chin, and throat, considered a defense against desires to suck, bite, or yell.

Reich is known for his classic work on character analysis, and for his formulations on the etiology, psychodynamics, and treatment of character neuroses. But threaded throughout his writing, somewhere between the more traditional formulations that are widely accepted by psychoanalysts and the mystical and much-ridiculed speculations of his later research on orgone energy, is a wealth of writing on the psychology of body movement. Alexander Lowen has extended Reich's "body" research, presenting rich clinical examples of muscle tensions, postures, and breathing patterns of neurotic and schizoid personalities (1958, 1967), and he has integrated the Reichian analysis of muscle armoring with recent concepts from ego psychology. (See Appendix I for further descriptions of Lowen's and Reich's work.) Christiansen (1963), a Norwegian psychologist influenced by Reich, has pointed out in a scholarly analysis of recent movement literature how various studies corroborate Reich, and has himself conducted research on breathing patterns that gives experimental support to some of Reich's ideas.

Beyond the work of Reich, Lowen, and Christiansen on movement and personality, one must go to an unusual source for a major study—a book written by a dance educator trained in movement analysis that extensively analyzes the relationships between the movement styles of school children and personality assessments (North, 1972). (See also Appendix I.) While individual differences in motor ability, muscle tension, gesture patterns, visual behavior, etc. have been noted by diverse researchers for a long time (cf. Gesell and Ames, 1937; Deutsch, 1949; Duffy, 1946; Kendon and Cook, 1969; Swan, 1938), the works of Allport and Vernon, Reich, Lowen, and now North represent the most comprehensive treatments of the subject.

PSYCHOLOGICAL INTERPRETATION OF SPECIFIC ACTIONS

Freud considered many "chance acts" to be indications of unconscious attitudes (Freud, 1938). He presumed that behaviors such as fidgeting in a particular way, bumping into someone on the street, and washing one's hands ritualistically have psychological significance.

In the 1930's a non-psychoanalytic psychologist, Maurice Krout, initiated a series of experiments designed to study the incidence and significance of various "autistic" gestures (e.g., types of fidgeting, self-touch, mannerisms while listening). Krout observed the movements of students in the classroom and in experimental situations. He accumulated lists of the observed behaviors, worked on problems of classification and reliability, analyzed "modal interpretations" of the gestures, and attempted to experimentally induce and assess the significance of various gestures (Krout 1931, 1935, 1954b). He found some consistent associations between movements and attitudes—fist gestures with aggression, hand to nose movements with fear, finger on lips with shame. He also found marked individual and sex differences in what gestures were performed.

In the late 1940's the psychoanalyst Felix Deutsch (1947, 1949) began a long study of the "postures" (actually positions or movements of the head, body, and limbs) of analytic patients on the couch. Making copious diagrams and notes of the patient's actions and the accompanying verbal themes, he evolved what he called "analytic posturology," theories of the symbolic significance of various movements and positions, particularly as they reflect unconscious conflicts about sexual identity, aggression, or dependency. In many instances Deutsch associated the gestures with very specific meanings (e.g., hands under the neck with guilt over masturbation); in some cases the movements immediately preceded early memories; and in some examples the rigidity or sameness of the position was regarded as a bad prognostic sign. Deutsch (1947) found that his patients had characteristic postures, individual "repertoires" of positions and movements that in a successful analysis became progressively freer and more variable.

Mahl has conducted exploratory studies of the gestures and postural shifts of patients during psychotherapy, attempting through more systematic research to investigate what Deutsch studied clinically (Mahl, 1968). Observing a patient's movements without sound, he tried to predict their significance and made interpretations as to the patient's psychodiagnosis, main areas of conflict, the affects he was expressing, his principle modes of defense, and so on. Mahl's predictions were often startlingly corroborated by clinical data. Like Krout, Mahl found marked individual and sex differences in the gestures and positions of his subjects. He presents a theoretical analysis of the situations in which nonverbal behavior anticipates latent associations that become verbalized minutes later. As a further argument for the unconscious determination of nonverbal behavior, Mahl cites instances in which a patient's dreams contained representations of actions actually observed in analysis (Mahl,

1968, p. 329). Mahl argues that there is a need for more study of the intrapsychic aspects of "transitory" actions; he says that such study is overshadowed in the literature on the one hand by attention to "chronic" nonverbal behaviors (cf. Reich) and on the other hand by research into regulatory and interpersonal aspects of body motion (Scheflen and Birdwhistell, to be discussed). Considering that there are only three major studies along the lines that Mahl suggests (those of Krout, Deutsch, and Mahl himself), one would have to agree. The preliminary work of these authors suggests that specific actions, such as fidgeting, self-touch patterns, and leg movements while talking, may be important indicators of unconscious conflicts and psychodynamic themes and processes.

INTERACTION AND COMMUNICATION

In 1952 an obscure monograph was published in Louisville, Kentucky entitled *Introduction to Kinesics*. In it an elaborate terminology and set of notations for recording body movement are presented, but beyond its workbook character one can discern a radically different theoretical approach to the study of body movement. Its author was Ray L. Birdwhistell, an anthropologist who has been deeply influenced by structural linguistics. Over the years, Birdwhistell came to eschew the "expressionist" bias in movement research, the tendency to see movement as reflecting inner states of emotion or attitude and the assumption that movement is somehow a kind of psychosomatic body language whose "meanings" are universally understood. Birdwhistell (1970) argues that body movement is simply one culturally determined "channel" of communication, that movement patterns are learned through social experience, and that one moves in ways commensurate with one's culture, social roles, region, age, sex, class, etc. He coined the term "kinesics" to refer to cultural-communicational study of body motion. Paramount in Birdwhistell's radical departure from earlier literature on body movement is his view that movement patterns are part of communication systems or programs. While there have been a few isolated studies of the development of social behaviors (e.g., Buhler, 1933), and the communicational significance of body motion had been acknowledged as far back as Darwin, no one till Birdwhistell gave such researches primary attention. Birdwhistell goes so far as to say that the "meaning" of a given movement can be deduced only from an analysis of the context—i.e., who does it, where, when, and within what sequence of interactions. The analogy here is to language decoding. When one hears a foreign language and must decipher it without assistance, he cannot assume that any of the sounds "mean" what he associates with these sounds in his own language. He must decipher the language through a process of comparing and contrasting sounds, determining when a given sound or sequence of sounds occurs, in what contexts, and in what combinations with other sounds, until he has found the units of meaningful sounds and understands how they combine into larger and larger units (words, phrases, sentences, etc.). In assuming that body motion is composed of small culturally determined units combining in hierarchies of larger and larger units, Birdwhistell is arguing that there is no "inherent" meaning to a movement, that its significance can be deciphered only from a "cracking" of the communication code, an understanding of the rules for combining and ordering various communicational behaviors. This implies that the relationship between the form or character of the movement and its meaning(s) is essentially arbitrary. Birdwhistell also dispensed with assumptions that different areas of the body express different things; that any one body part or type of movement was "more communicative" than any other; and that movement can be studied in isolation irrespective of other channels such as verbal, olfactory, or tactile ones. In his view, social interaction does not follow an A then B then A action-reaction pattern such as A talks and conveys information, then B talks, then A talks, but is characterized by a complex orchestration of several channels at once with feedback and regulation going on continuously.

There are a number of practical ramifications of his theoretical position. Birdwhistell does not study the face or any other body area in isolation, nor does he utilize observer interpretation of a movement's significance. In Birdwhistell's framework what a person judges a movement or facial display to mean may simply reflect what culture he is from. He also eschews experimental research on movement as artificially isolating and intruding on the natural phenomena and thereby effecting new and rather unusual programs of communication. Kinesics research typically involves elaborate study of films at slow motion. The camera is optimally set on the entire bodies of all subjects for the entire period to be studied. While Birdwhistell's writing spans 20 years of work and is largely theoretical, one can cull from it a number of empirical observations and findings such as the complex interplay of behaviors between a mother and infant that can occur during 1.75 seconds; courtship patterns and "gender displays" among American adolescents; and some specific relationships between motion and verbal syntax—e.g., forward gestures with future tense, posterior movements with past tense (Birdwhistell, 1970, pp. 19-23, 44-45, 124). While it is rarely clear how often or consistently a particular pattern has been observed, Birdwhistell's data are rich with promise. Some of the observations of Birdwhistell and his colleague Scheflen may well become established as important original discoveries in behavioral research, particularly their analyses of the intricacies of interaction patterns. (See Appendix I for additional discussions of the work of Birdwhistell and Scheflen.)

Scheflen, a psychiatrist with psychoanalytic training, joined Birdwhistell some years ago, recognizing the value of starting fresh and not applying an old framework like psychoanalytic theory to what was becoming a burgeoning research area—direct, minute study of small-group interaction through films. Rather than isolating specific parameters for study, he and Birdwhistell evolved a kind of disciplined naturalistic observation procedure that Scheflen calls "context analysis." Through it one studies what behaviors continually recur, in what combinations, and in what contexts. Scheflen devoted several years to the minute analysis of a thirty-minute family psychotherapy film (1965). Eventually he seemed to "crack" the interaction code, showing how the four group members were involved in a complex series of behaviors, with smaller units of behavior combining into progressively larger units and with regular oscillations at each level. Scheflen delineates elaborate "regulatory" behaviors (many of them nonverbal) that serve to maintain or redirect the interaction, and discovers complementary and reciprocal performances that sustain group cohesion. He deciphers some of the rules, mechanisms, and procedures by which the face-to-face interaction is organized. Perhaps most notable is his contention that the "program" may be maintained irrespective of the individuals involved. After 23 minutes everyone could be seen to shift roles—for example, the mother and daughter switched roles, with one therapist gradually assuming the mother's place in the group and the other therapist taking the place of the first (Scheflen, 1965, p. 122). If in fact such a process of "musical chairs" can occur, this can be considered support for the argument that these nonverbal behaviors are essentially social not individual.

In practical terms Scheflen has concentrated on larger units of behavior than Birdwhistell, in a sense delineating the sentences, paragraphs, and chapters of body motion (cf. his terms "point," "position," and "presentation"), while Birdwhistell's research stays at the level of variations occurring within 1-3 seconds. But Scheflen shares Birdwhistell's contention that body motion should be considered part of the social communication system. He defines communication as:

> a cultural system consisting of successive levels of patterning that support, amend, modify, define and make possible human (and maybe animal) relationships. We cannot *see* human relationships or social structures. What we see are the *communicative activities that maintain and signify them.* (Scheflen, 1965, p. 17)

Birdwhistell and Scheflen represent the major proponents of a strictly communicational focus on body motion—i.e., they criticize the imputation of intrapsychic or individual meanings to movement (at least until the cultural and interactional patterns are delineated). A number of researchers have been directly influenced by them, particularly Condon and Ogston (1967) and Kendon (1972). Condon and Ogston (1967) have shown how body movements between individuals or between an individual and his own speech may be highly synchronous at the "micro" level that Birdwhistell concentrates on. Kendon (1972) presents an impressive analysis of how movements of different body parts correspond to different units of speech. He found that "the larger the speech unit, the more body parts there are that are involved in" the "speech-preparatory movement" (Kendon, 1972, p. 205). Duncan (1970) has analyzed the complex nonverbal behaviors that regulate "floor apportionment"—who speaks in conversation and when.

Other researchers may not strictly adhere to a communicational approach, but many do reflect the shift from "expressive," intra-psychic interpretations, to a focus on social factors in body motion. For example, Argyle and Dean (1965) found that the amount of eye contact decreases as subjects sit closer; and Exline et al. (1961) found that subjects who had cheated showed decreased "visual interaction." Mehrabian (1968) has investigated the ways subjects stand in relation to persons of different status, age, sex, and likeability. The focus on the social and communicative aspects of movement appears to predominate at present; it is clear that Birdwhistell initiated a major new direction in research on body motion.

CULTURAL COMPARISONS

The study of cultural differences in body movement was anticipated by Darwin but it remained virtually an unexplored area for many years by all but dance ethnologists. There is a rich literature on various dances and rituals performed around the world (e.g., Kurath, 1960) and within this a great deal of insight into the relations between dance styles, group organization, and social mores. Although one can find scattered references to gesture conventions, facial expressions, ceremonials, etc. in anthropological writing, concentrated study of cultural differences in body movement is rare until Efron's (1941) classic analysis of the differences between Italian and Jewish gestural behavior.

Efron himself was a Jew from Argentina studying anthropology in New York City. He presented a study of the effects of acculturation on gestures as a refutation of some German anti-semitic literature arguing that certain gestures and body types were racially determined and innate. Efron and his artist colleague spent two years observing, describing, and drawing the gestures, group formations, and touch patterns of first and second generation Italians and Jews in New York City. He observed people talking in clusters on the Lower East Side or in social gatherings on the West Side. He noted that first generation Jews tended to stand much closer together, move the lower arms and hands, create elaborate paths in space as they gestured, and touch each other continually. First generation Italians tended to stand farther apart, gesture with large, whole arm units, use more mime-like gestures punctuated with vigorous sweeps, and rarely touch each other. While the differences between the first generation Jews and Italians were numerous and interesting, their children began to resemble each other and to move like middle class Americans. (See also Appendix I.)

Efron's study is very frequently cited in recent literature; it remains virtually alone, however, except for a few other studies. Most notably, LaBarre (1947) has reported differences in gestures around the world. Hewes (1955) has analyzed "postural habits" cross-culturally from photographs and literature. Birdwhistell cites some examples of kinesic differences between people of different geographic regions (Birdwhistell, 1970, pp. 208-11); he, of course, argues that movement is largely culturally variable. Hall (1966) has written on cultural differences in proximity and touch, initiating a new research area he calls "proxemics." He has found, for example, that Arabs tend to stand closer together when they talk than Englishmen do (Hall, 1966). The study of proximity may, of course, be seen as a part of movement research, dealing as it does with group formations.

In 1966 a team of researchers, including a musicologist with years of experience in the cultural study of song style and dancers trained in

Laban's movement analysis systems, began an ambitious cross-cultural study of dance and work styles using anthropological films from around the world (Lomax, Bartenieff, and Paulay, 1968). They devised coding sheets useful in recording the elements of movement style of homogeneous, non-industrialized cultures. What emerges from this research, called choreometrics, is a picture of the astounding degree to which the movement styles correlate with the socioeconomic subsistence levels of the cultures. That is, the level of complexity of the movement styles (as measured, for example, by the type of spatial transition from simple reversal to three-dimensional looped transitions from one direction to another) correlates with the level of economic complexity, from simple gatherers to agriculturalists with irrigation (Lomax et al., 1968, p. 242). They also found that they could divide the world into eight regions according to dance style and that from their coding sheets they could derive movement profiles illustrating the differences and similarities between various cultures. Since choreometrics concentrates on style, it is not limited to dance analysis; the coding can as readily be done on work movement patterns and presumably on movement characteristics observed in social gatherings. While the field is rapidly advancing beyond the original findings on the relationships between socioeconomic levels and movement styles, the original book remains important here as a major study of large cultural differences in movement patterns. (See Appendix I for further discussion of choreometrics.)

Staying at a global level, there are a few studies of note. Eibl-Eibesfeldt has found that an eyebrow raise and smile occur in greetings of widely different cultures (1971). And, as mentioned, Ekman et al. (1969) have found that certain facial expressions are universally identified across literate and non-literate cultures. In a sense these studies can be seen as evidence of pan-cultural, or what used to be called "universal," aspects of body motion and its recognition.

DEVELOPMENTAL PATTERNS

Finally, it is appropriate here to consider the literature on the developmental aspects of nonverbal communication or expressive movement. Again it is notable that Darwin analyzed the development of facial expressions in his young children, a subject extensively examined by Spitz (1946) in his analysis of the emergence of the smiling response, and by Washburn (1929) in her study of developmental stages in expressive behavior in the first year of life. In the 1920's and 1930's there were a number of studies of infants and nursery children that included observations of nonverbal expressions (cf. Buhler, 1933) and considerable attention has been given in the last 20 years to the direct observation of mother-infant interactions, much of the analysis of course focusing on nonverbal behavior (Levy, 1958). However, while Birdwhistell (1970) argues that the development of kinesic patterns is a highly complex cultural process, we have very little actual data on when certain gestures and expressions occur, let alone on how a child becomes an active member of a communication "program" such as is described by Scheflen.

A few psychoanalysts have considered the role of movement in the development of ego mechanisms and in character formation, notably Spitz (1957) in his psychoanalytic treatment of the ontogenesis of head-shaking from the rooting response of the neonate to a semantic signal of negation, and Mittlemann's postulation of a distinct motor phase of ego development around age two (Mittlemann, 1954). But of particular interest here is the work of Kestenberg and her colleagues on the role of body movement in development. Kestenberg (1965) integrates many years of detailed observations of children's movement patterns with Laban's approach to movement analysis and with Freudian theory. She focuses on minute fluctuations in "tension flow" and "shape flow" (roughly similar to observable variations in muscle tension and in patterns of expanding and contracting in space). While much of her work requires an understanding of Laban's effort-shape analysis, as when she says the newborn has no "effort" qualities in his movement, a number of her observations can be understood without it. Kestenberg maintains that there are individual differences in movement patterns from birth (as does Fries, 1938) and that these congenital motor rhythms persist throughout the child's development, though they become modified and more complex (Kestenberg, 1965). Further, she finds that although a child may have certain "preferred rhythms" that are important expressions of his personality, every child goes through stages of development where certain rhythms relate to and serve specific drive discharge. She delineates "sinosoidal" curves of tension flow as characteristic of the oral stage, and goes on to describe anal, urethral, and phallic rhythms of movement tension. She also extends her analysis to a consideration of the relationship of the development of rhythms and spatial dimension factors to cognitive and affective stages (Kestenberg et al., 1972). For example, she finds that a predominance of "urethral" rhythms, growing control over starting, running, and stopping, and stress on the sagittal plane (the forward and backward dimension) are some motor correlates of the phase during which the child is developing time constancy concepts.

A great deal of research on movement development deals with the normal states of growth of posture, locomotion, and visual-prehensile behavior. In the 1930's Gesell and his colleagues did elaborate film analyses of when the child focused, grasped, rolled over, stood up, etc. (Gesell and Halverson, 1942; Halverson, 1931), and McGraw (1943) wrote a classic analysis of the stages in motor development as they reflect neuromuscular maturation. While it was assumed that in some way the level of motor development reflected the child's general developmental progress (developmental scales for infants and toddlers include many motor tests), research on the relationships between motor ability and general intelligence remains inconclusive.

CONCLUDING REMARKS

For a closer look at some of the most important research surveyed here—ones that will be discussed and used in subsequent chapters of this thesis—the reader is referred to Appendix I. Table I illustrates that the history of movement research follows a general progression from a concentration on movement's emotional and psychophysiological dimensions, to an anlysis of intrapsychic personality correlates of body motion, to an emphasis on interpersonal and cultural aspects of movement. That is, one can virtually draw a line from the upper left corner to the lower right of the Table, from the stress on physiological and affect aspects of movement to a gradual emergence of communication and interaction studies. In this sense movement research mirrors the progress of behavioral research in general over this century. But while these phases reflect scientific vogues, there is relatively little supplanting of one focus by another. It is, as the chart illustrates, a gradual expansion, an inclusion of new correlations and findings. Today there are prominent "movement researchers" in all of the areas defined in this history, and unlike the earlier periods, they now seem more and more in communication with each other, recognizing that at least to an extent all their work falls under the rubric of body motion research (whether it is called nonverbal communication, kinesics, expressive movement, body language, etc.) and that this subject now covers the entire area from developmental to cross-cultural studies. While previously a great deal of work was done in isolation (sometimes, it seems, by people who pursued it simply out of

TABLE 1

HISTORICAL PERSPECTIVE OF MOVEMENT RESEARCH

	Pre - 1900	1900-1930	1930's	1940's	1950's	1960's ⟶
Developmental Patterns	Darwin		Gesell--------⟶ Halverson Washburn Buhler	McGraw Spitz------⟶	Mittelmann------⟶	Kestenberg
Emotion	Darwin	James-Lange Landis Ruckmick	Jenness Goodenough Luria Jacobsen---------		Schlosberg Frijda, Bull, Malmo ------------⟶	Ekman et al.
Personality and Psychopathology	Darwin Bleuler	Ferenczi	Allport & Vernon Reich------- Fries	W. Wolff C. Wolff	Lowen------⟶ ------------⟶	Christiansen North Davis
Psychological Interpretation of Specific Actions		Freud	Krout		Deutsch	Mahl
Interaction and Communication			Buhler		Birdwhistell-----⟶ Kurath Hewes	Scheflen Condon, Duncan Kendon, Loeb Argyle Exline Mehrabian Hall
Cultural Comparisons	Darwin			LaBarre Efron	Birdwhistell-----⟶	Lomax, Bar- tenieff, & Paulay Eibl-Eibesfeldt Ekman

27

private conviction and enthusiasm), today there is an increasing cross-fertilization of approaches and findings (Davis, 1972).

One can only speculate on why the subject has had so few major contributions until now. World War II appears to have cut short the burgeoning psychological research on movement of the 1920's and 1930's. It seems that the practical application of movement analysis—e.g., in intelligence tests or psychodiagnostic tests—never materialized sufficiently to give it research priority. While Luria may have seen its potential for lie detection in 1932 and government agencies may be interested now in the value of nonverbal communication research in determining what an ally or enemy "really means" at a conference, it is still a largely "non-applied" area of research. The sheer complexity and subtlety of body movement seems to militate against its being narrowed to concrete, duplicatable tests and measurements.

In spite of its elusiveness, movement appears to be enjoying a renaissance of research attention. It seems that there is a perceptible frustration with the limitation of words that encourages movement research. The growth of group and family psychotherapy with increased use of videotape and film has encouraged clinicians and researchers to consider the importance of the continual body motion of people in face-to-face interaction. Of course those who have problems with language as a primary source of information about their subjects, such as anthropologists in the field, ethologists watching primates, or psychologists studying young infants, must attend a great deal to nonverbal behavior. Given these obvious reasons for the current "movement movement," one can only wonder at the profound cultural and philosophical factors underlying the neglect of a subject having such obvious potential for granting new insights into human behavior.

Chapter III

DRAWING ON MOVEMENT NOTATION SYSTEMS FOR A GLOSSARY OF MOVEMENT TERMS

A SURVEY OF THREE NOTATION SYSTEMS

In an empirical study it is important to define exactly what behavior one is considering, and this is nowhere more apparent than in movement research. Most of the research described in Chapter II showed problems of movement description and greatly needed sound, operational definitions of whatever the investigator was observing. In this field one film is worth a thousand words. Using simple language such as "he scratched his nose" is, in effect, so inadequate that one has to take a great many of the research findings on "blind" faith because one cannot be sure exactly what behavior the researcher is talking about. A person can scratch (rub? wipe? touch?) his nose (to the side? underneath? above?) with his hand (alone? as part of a whole arm movement? open or closed? etc.) in many different ways. One source for the systematic, logical, and comprehensive movement terminology that is so sorely needed in behavioral research of movement is dance or movement notation systems. This chapter will be devoted to a consideration of certain systems for recording movement from the point of view of their value for providing concepts and terms for analyzing movement.

The systems for describing and recording body movement that will be surveyed in this chapter developed historically quite separately from the research discussed previously. For the most part psychologists and anthropologists have used their own terminology and techniques for observing and recording movement. Dance ethnologists sometimes turn to dance notations for recording techniques (Kurath, 1960). And, of course, research influenced by Rudolf Laban adapts his techniques. But for the most part behavioral researchers have not studied these systems to see what value they might have. A notable exception is Birdwhistell, who reports that he studied Labanotation and decided to develop his own system of kinesic analysis instead, although he advises students to use Laban's for certain areas of investigation. Birdwhistell remarks, "I have chosen not to use Labanotation as an investigatory tool for communication analysis . . . It seems to me that it assumed that which I wish to investigate." (Birdwhistell, 1970, p. 256). Ekman and Friesen appear to reject movement notation systems in their discussion of a taxonomy for nonverbal acts:

> The classification of acts and positions is thus based upon what is easily recognizable to any observer . . . No notational system or series of measurements is needed to distinguish between movements or to recall types of acts or positions; instead a simple verbal label is utilized. (1968, p. 194)

However, these are rare, passing remarks in the literature; the question is still very much open to debate.

What follows is an overview and comparison of different movement notation systems. Each originated from dance analysis and then was found to be applicable to any type of movement. Three systems have been chosen here, although there are a number of well-developed notation systems that may be of use in behavioral research (see Appendix II). The reasons for choosing Labanotation, Eshkol-Wachmann, and Laban's Effort-Shape Analysis are that (1) they are widely recognized and extensively developed; (2) they appear to be rather different from each other and, considered altogether, cover the broadest range of movement terms and concepts; and (3) there is already considerable evidence of their research value (see Appendix II). As will be seen, each system "cuts the pie" differently—i.e., each focuses on different aspects of movement or on the same aspects in slightly different ways, so that each would describe and record the same movement differently. At the end of this chapter these differences will be illustrated by a presentation of how each system would describe a movement that is widely known—President Nixon's raised-arms greeting to crowds.

It is important to mention here that the author has had formal training in the Laban systems and feels more secure in using them; the treatment of the Eshkol-Wachmann system has been done from a study of their textbook (Eshkol and Wachmann, 1958), admittedly an inadequate preparation.

The following does not purport to be a thorough presentation of the systems, intensive study of the textbooks and formal training are required to fully understand them. The reader is referred to Appendix II for an annotated bibliography of technical writing on notations that may be of value to researchers interested in pursuing the subject in depth. Each system will be briefly introduced and then various terms and concepts will be selected to be presented in chart form. The chart will illustrate how many variables one can choose to focus on in a study of nonverbal behavior.

Labanotation

A discussion of Labanotation will provide a good introduction to the field of dance notation and how it may be used and developed. Labanotation was invented by Rudolf Laban, a choreographer who spent a lifetime exploring movement and the problems of analyzing it. Labanotation (or Kinetography Laban) has been tested, refined, and developed for over 50 years. It is, of course, mainly used for recording dances, thereby preserving them and making reconstruction possible. While dance notation may be to dance what music notation is to music, dance notation has evolved much more slowly, and choreographers rarely use it when they first write down their works, unlike music composers. Rather, a dance work is choreographed and then a dance notator may be called in to record the dance from repeated observations (usually watching rehearsals). Notating a dance is an enormous undertaking (imagine deriving a music score of Beethoven's Fifth by repeated listening) and requires extensive formal training. Work done by one notator is checked by another and revisions and refinements are made until the notated score is deemed accurate, logical, and sufficiently true to the work that it can be read by someone who has never seen the dance but who knows the notation. This means that it must be complete enough for the dance to be reproduced from the score itself. Labanotation has been greatly developed over the years in Europe and the United States. In fact, experts in the notation are in continual communication, thrashing out technical problems, notation conventions, and theoretical issues in analyzing movement; and there is an international conclave that meets to discuss such matters. For many years these experts have recognized the value of Labanotation for recording all forms of movement and have striven to extend its application beyond the specialized recording of dance forms.

The notation itself is based on a vertical staff, with devisions for time intervals and columns for movements of different body parts. There are "notes" that vary in length, shape, and shading according to the duration, direction, and level of the movement. Columns for weight placement make it possible to indicate where and how the weight is supported, and other columns are so arranged that one can see at a glance what body parts are moving, in what combinations, in what directions, and for how long. There are additional symbols for details of the body, degrees of contraction and extension, patterns of touch, group formations, various relationships between movers, and many more. Its scope can only be alluded to here; the reader is referred to the textbook on Labanotation by Ann Hutchinson (1970) to appreciate the extent and refinement of the system. It is important here to point out that Labanotation represents not only a set of symbols for efficient recording, but a body of concepts and terms for describing movement; it is these concepts that will be considered subsequently.

Eshkol-Wachmann Movement Notation

The Eshkol-Wachmann system differs radically from Labanotation. Developed in the early 1950's by two Israelis, it was first applied and tested by Noa Eshkol for her dance group. However, since then it has been used to record such diverse movements as animal actions, deaf sign language, and Indian gestures (see Appendix II). The system sets out to record the "formal aspect of the relations and *changes* of *relations* between the parts of the body" (Eshkol and Wachmann, 1958, p. 5) in terms of which parts move, the angular relationship between the "real" and "imaginary" axes of the moving part, and careful attention to the degree and direction of the movement. It is perhaps the closest of the movement notations to a geometrical analysis of joint action and spatial patterns. Three types of movement are defined: a "rotatory" movement in which a limb moves about its axis, a "plane" movement in which the "longitudinal axis of the moving limb describes a plane" and a "curved" movement in which "the longitudinal axis of the moving limb describes a curved surface" usually a conical shape (p. 6).

The analysis is made relative to a zero position (normal standing), to horizontal and vertical planes, and to the relation of the limbs to various "systems of reference." Any movement can be described as some series and combination of these possibilities. The degree of movement and the direction in terms of clock-wise or counter-clockwise are noted. The notation itself consists of a series of numbers, symbols, and arrows placed on a 20-row graph, the rows representing different body parts and the horizontal units representing duration. Further distinctions are made for movements describing non-circular paths: elliptical, undulatory, and spiral.

Effort-Shape Analysis

The principle symbols of both Labanotation and Eshkol-Wachmann may be seen as analogous to the notes and bars of music notation—i.e., path or direction in space is comparable to pitch and tone in music, duration of the movement to duration of the note, and simultaneity of body parts moving in various directions to chords in music. There are special aspects of movement that have no clear counterparts in music, such as weight placement, but, roughly speaking, the spatial or "structural" analyses of Labanotation and Eshkol-Wachmann are analogous to the formal, tonal aspects of music. Just as dynamic remarks are added to the music score, a notation may add "dynamic" or qualitative details as modifiers or qualifiers to the "spatial event." Labanotation adds dynamic or accent marks beside the score such as for strong and tremolo (Hutchinson, 1970, p. 509).

Consider, however, a system in which the quality, intensity, and dynamic pattern of the movement is primary and the "structural" aspect secondary. In this system "how" becomes the figure and "where, when, which body part" becomes the ground. Effort-Shape analysis is such a system. It provides a way of analyzing the qualitative and intensity aspects of movement. Its origins go back to Laban's early work in the 1920's, but it became formalized as an analysis system of its own in the 1950's through Laban's studies of work skill (Laban and Lawrence, 1947). His colleague Warren Lamb has developed the system further (Lamb, 1969) and another colleague Marion North has developed the complex theories of interpretation that Laban evolved with his "Effort Analysis" (North, 1972).

Effort-Shape analysis describes how a movement is performed in terms of combinations and sequences of effort qualities—slow or quick, light or strong, indirect or direct; in terms of the "effort flow" characteristics (variations in free or uncontrolled, and bound or controlled movement); and in terms of how the movement projects through space—shape flow (simply toward or away from the body), directional movement (projection toward a goal or clear direction), or shaping (projecting into space with the creation of three-dimensional forms of the body and of the space described) (Bartenieff and Davis, 1965). It is perhaps helpful to imagine a focus that highlights the crescendoes and decrescendoes, the patterns of clarity or vagueness, the fluctuations in rhythm of a movement while its formal directions or content (what is done) are background.

Effort-Shape is considered a system complementary to Labanotation although they evolved separately at different times. Unlike the other systems, Effort-Shape has not been applied primarily to dance analysis. It has so far been adapted to behavioral studies of child development (Kestenberg, 1965); cultural differences in movement style (Lomax, Bartenieff, and Paulay, 1968); individual movement styles (Bartenieff and Davis, 1965); and psychopathological aspects of body movement (Davis, 1970). Consequently its concepts are used in check sheets and scales, but it is not commonly used as a notation system per se.

The following table shows how each system might describe the same movement in a slightly different way. The movement is the gesture President Nixon sometimes makes when he victoriously salutes a crowd by raising both arms over his head. It is important to remember that this is a movement and not simply a position. Even held positions have active characteristics such as a heightened tension or a sustained direction.

DEVELOPMENT OF A MOVEMENT GLOSSARY

Each movement analysis system is based on certain fundamental concepts and categories—for example, direction, spatial planes, weight placement, and so on—and a movement is analyzed according to combinations and sequences of particular variables. Considering the systems as sources of categories and parameters, one can derive a list or glossary of movement terms potentially valuable for research. As stated earlier the three systems selected for attention here seem collectively to cover the widest range of terms. It is of course entirely possible that other systems include categories not considered in these and that new developments in notation will yield new parameters. However, at present these appear to be good sources for an extensive movement glossary or lexicon, one which will no doubt require continual additions and revisions.

The "movement glossary" that follows has evolved in part from the author's experience in research (which has been greatly influenced by a study of Labanotation and Laban's Effort-Shape Analysis) and from an

TABLE 2

*THREE ANALYSES OF THE SAME MOVEMENT**

Labanotation:

Standing in place, facing the audience, he rapidly raises both arms forward-side-middle to side-high, his hands rotated outward to a side-middle position, palms facing place-high, fingers together. His head moves forward. There is a brief hold of this total position.

Eshkol-Wachmann:

Standing in Zero Position, facing front, he raises both arms in a plane movement traversing 180 degrees in an intermediate plane, resulting in a final position (a) with a rotated state of (b) for the arms and a (c) position of the hands and a (d) position of the head. (a, b, c, and d refer to specific numbers for vertical and horizontal coordinates relative to the "system of reference"; see Eshkol-Wachmann, p. 55).

Effort-Shape Analysis:

Both arms (moved as whole units) are raised upward, forward and outward directionally in a postural movement that is at first quick and strong then held bound. The head is forward, shoulders are narrow, arms and hands are outward, and fingers are closed, representing a combination of opposing shape flow tendencies: out-in-out-in.

---

* No claim is made for the technical accuracy of these descriptions. They were done by the author from a book-study of the systems and so are not "official." It is hoped that they are at least fair indicators of differences in terminology and focus among the three systems. These differences would be even more dramatic if it were possible to present the notations as well.

examination of the three systems for purposes of developing a glossary. Textbooks on Labanotation (e.g., that of Hutchinson, 1970), Eshkol-Wachmann (Eshkol and Wachmann, 1958), and Effort-Shape Analysis (e.g., Dell, 1970) are organized according to general movement categories and one can examine such works for a list of concepts and terms as has been done here. It is, however, not always possible to state how and from where a glossary term has been drawn in each instance. When a concept is shared by more than one system, it is simply listed and defined. When a term is unique to a given system, the initials of the system are indicated in parenthesis: Ln for Labanotation, E-W for Eshkol-Wachmann, and E-S for Effort-Shape Analysis. When a term is a special one that appears to be coined within a given system, it may be put in quotes. However, the selection of certain terms and such additional distinctions as are listed at the end of the glossary have been influenced by the author's research experience or literature review. For example, categories such as "body attitude" and "transition" may be found in the literature on Laban's systems, but their importance has really been established by the choreometrics research of Lomax, Bartenieff, and Paulay (1968).

The definitions and examples have been written by the author and are not to be considered "official"; exact technical definitions can be found in the literature cited in Appendix II. In some cases a movement feature may not be directly defined or notated but one can see it "embedded" in the system or can derive it from an examination of the notation. For example, "synchrony" is continually notated by the systems simply because simultaneous movements of different parts or of two movers are written next to each other. But it is not explicitly discussed very much.

As has been illustrated with the Nixon example, each system may analyze the same features differently. In some cases there also may be important differences in definition of the same term. For example, "light" in Eshkol-Wachmann refers to parts that are passively moved (Eshkol and Wachmann, 1958, p. 24), while "light" in Effort-Shape Analysis means an active quality of airiness or weightlessness (Dell, 1970, p. 21). It is not appropriate here to go into such technical considerations as these. They are of importance to specialists in the systems and perhaps to researchers grappling with exact definitions. But for the purposes of this thesis, it is sufficient to consider the principal concepts and terms of the systems and to present them in a non-technical way.

MOVEMENT GLOSSARY

I. *Held or Maintained Aspects*

    A.   Body attitude or posture: the character of one's general stance; the way the torso, head and body are carried—as in someone moving with a continually erect, vertical posture. This is a broad item that can be described in many ways.

    B.   Position: still arrangements of body parts in relation to each other, types of contact between parts, and possibly the spatial configurations of the limbs, head, and trunk—for example, hands resting on the lap with fingers intertwined.

    C.   Hold: some feature is held, movement stopped, no change.

II. *Mobile Aspects*

    A.   Body parts

        1.   Entire body: focus on movement of any and every body part although this may vary in degree of detail from highly refined (such as smallest finger movements) to fairly gross units (such as upper limbs).

        2.   Selective: concentration on specific parts (while essentially not attending to others).

            a) head—as in head nodding, turning

            b) upper limbs: hands and fingers, lower arms, arms as a unit—as in hand gesticulations while speaking

            c) lower limbs: feet alone, lower legs, leg as a unit—as in foot tapping

            d) trunk: shifts of the trunk, movement within the trunk—such as leaning back in a chair

            e) facial movements or expressions*: may be described in terms of areas of the face articulated, direction of facial movement, degree of expansion, etc.

        3.   Visual Behavior

            a) eye contact with, or visual regard of, another person

            b) visual focus and coordination per se—e.g., steady visual regard of an object as one walks by it (Ln)

        4.   Surface areas of body—e.g., palm, sole of foot, etc. (Ln)

        5.   Types of relationships between body parts

            a) successive spreading of movement from one part to the next vs. simultaneous movement, all parts at once (Ln)

            b) unilateral vs. bilateral—e.g., one arm gesticulates while the other is still vs. both arms gesturing together in the same way

c) synchronous: parts begin to move or change direction together

d) right-left distinctions: note as to whether the movement is on the right side or the left

e) initiating or leading part—e.g., the movement actively begins in one part and is followed by other parts

f) active vs. passive movement: some parts may be passively moved as a result of active movement in another area or because of outside forces

6. Gesture-posture (E-S): movement involving only part of the body is called gestural in E-S; movement which actively engages the entire body is called postural.

B. Spatial Aspects

1. Areas of space: the reach space around the mover; one's "kinesphere" (Ln) in terms of areas above, back of, in front of, etc. the mover.

2. In-out dimension: general contraction or expansion, "growing-shrinking" (E-S), "concave-convex" (E-W); movement going inward or outward.

3. Direction: specific directions relative to the mover and his own body axis—e.g., sideward and upward relative to his front (E-S), or relative to outside points—e.g., side high (Ln).

4. Planes and planal stress: the planes in which movement occurs either in terms of two (horizontal and vertical) or three (horizontal, vertical, and sagittal); what plane(s) are generally stressed or emphasized.

5. "Plane movement": the moving limb describes a plane (E-W).

6. Types of path or "trace form" (Ln): the character of the lines in space drawn by the tip of the moving part—such as straight, curved, or zig zag.

7. Two- or three-dimensional figures in space—e.g., the conical shape created by a circular movement of an extended arm (E-W) or "shaping" in E-S, which refers to sculpting in space three-dimensionally—e.g., when a mime gestures with a flourish as he bows, his arms often create a shaping movement.

8. Spatial transition: the character of the connection from one direction to another—e.g., an angular transition.

9. Size, range or extent of the movement—e.g., degrees of contraction or extension.
10. Qualitative terms

    a) vague to clear spatial form or projection through space (E-S): some movements appear vague, "formless," directionless in contrast to movements with a definite form and direction

    b) direct or indirect: "piercing" through space vs. distinctly sinuous or meandering (E-S)

C. Kinesiological Terms
   1. Flexion-extension: decreases or increases in joint angles without reference to space.
   2. Rotation: turning on the axis of the limb or part that is moving.

D. Tension-Related Terms
   1. Tense vs. relaxed: increased or decreased muscle tension.
   2. Effort flow (E-S): fluctuations of "free" and "bound" control, the fluency and ongoingness of the movement, as in freely running vs. readily "stoppable".[b]

E. Weight-Related Terms
   1. Support, weight placement: where and how the body is supported and the weight is placed—e.g., standing on one foot.
   2. Center of weight: at any moment there is an imaginary center of weight on which the body is poised or balanced; it varies with the body build, position, etc. (Ln).
   3. Weight shifts: shifting of the weight, particularly over the point of support.
   4. Qualitative Terms

      a) heavy: a quality of "mass" or weight—as in a sluggish gait

      b) forceful, strong (E-S)—as in punching or hammering

      c) light, weightless (E-S)—as in delicately brushing off a speck of dirt one doesn't want to smudge

      d) weak, tentative—e.g., a very old person who moves his cane tentatively without firmness or strength

      e) giving into gravity, "letting the weight go"—e.g., dropping limply into a chair

F. Time-Related Terms [c]
   1. Duration: the length of time a movement takes.
   2. Tempo: relative time a series of movements are performed at.
   3. Acceleration-deceleration: gradual increase or decrease in speed.
   4. Qualitative Terms
      a) quick, sudden (E-S)—e.g., a startle
      b) slow, sustained (E-S)—e.g., carefully picking up a full bowl of water
   5. Rhythmic synchrony or coordination: one body part maintains a pacing or tempo different from but related to that of another part—e.g., shaking one's head at four times the tempo at which one rocks back and forth.

G. Touch Patterns: may be described in terms of what body parts touch, where, and in what way (e.g., brush, grasp, support) (Ln); also may distinguish between touching oneself, an object, or another person.

H. Locomotion
   1. Types of turns—e.g., turns while standing in place, turns while walking, turns on one foot vs. from one foot to another, etc.
   2. Types of jumps—e.g., on same foot, both feet, etc.
   3. Types of steps—e.g., flat-footed, on ball of foot, on toes, weight distributed from heel to toe vs. all at once.
   4. Direction travelled or "floor pattern" (Ln)—e.g., walking straight from the door to a particular chair.
   5. Types of walk: a complex phenomenon that can be elabrately analyzed in terms of the posture sustained, the limb activity, how the foot is placed, etc. and how these are integrated, paced, and emphasized.

I. Group Relationship Terms
   1. Group formations: seating or standing arrangements—e.g., sitting all in a circle or standing scattered loosely throughout a room.
   2. Types of positioning or movement relationships between people.
      a) orientation—e.g., standing in front of, beside, or behind

another; facing or with back to someone

b) toward or away: movement toward or away from another

c) proximity, or nearness: the relative degree of closeness between people

d) symmetry: may be lateral, as when two people do the same movement or position but on opposite sides, or sagittal, as when one moves in the same way as another but the forward and backward dimensions are contrasting—i.e., A moves forward as B moves back (Ln)

e) opposition: where right and left are exchanged, as are forward and back (cf. the ballroom dancing relationship[d]) (Ln)

f) synchrony: easily determined from the movement "score" —e.g., two people begin to move or change direction at the same time or do the same movement at the same time

g) common "focal point" (Ln): two or more people move in relation to or orient themselves to a fixed point in the room—e.g., everyone turns and looks to the door or all gravitate towards a punch bowl

h) succession: one person does a movement, then the next person does the same, then a third, and so on

i) leading, following: one person appears to initiate a particular movement that others follow[e]

j) "floor plans" (Ln): general clusterings and movement paths of the group—e.g., all line up and go from one side of the room to the door

J. Pattern Features[f]

1. Constant or recurring characteristics[g]—e.g., stylistic features such as holding the head in a particular way throughout one's activity, as in the way Johnny Carson of TV fame characteristically holds his head vertically and somewhat back.

2. Movement phrases[h]: the pattern characteristics of specific movements—e.g., a pattern in which the intensity occurs at the beginning, as in a quick start in surprise followed by a gradual diminution of activity as the person "composes" himself, or a pattern in which the intensity builds to the end of the movement, as in hitting a table with maximum force and a hold at the end.

3. "Motifs": certain complex movement patterns involving combinations of features that may persist or recur throughout a series of variations—e.g., one can continually rock back and forth and shake one's head while performing a complex series of gestures.

4. "Composition": the overall organization of movers in relation to each other over time; the composition of their movement interaction, each having a voice that is synchronous, contrapuntal, interrelated in some way with each other such that the entire event has an organization and pattern —e.g., members of a football team may develop various formations and moves together that are a kind of composition of plays.

K. "Unit" Size or Length: the relative duration or size of the variables studied; the easiest way to consider this is in terms of actual duration:

1. 1/48 to 2 seconds—e.g., "micro" displacements in space such as are seen in slow motion film.

2. 2 to 15 seconds: movements occurring in relatively short sequences—as from the start to stop of a gesticulation.

3. 15 seconds to 2 minutes—such as positions that are held for a while.

4. 2 minutes to 30 minutes—e.g., the overall rate of postural shifts occurring in a brief psychotherapy session.

L. Amount or Frequency: the relative frequency of occurrence of the behavioral unit or action observed—e.g., the number of nose rub actions per five minutes.

---

[a] This is perhaps the least attended to in what are body movement notations. Notably, a system not reviewed here deals appreciably with analysis of facial expression (Morris, 1928).

[b] This is virtually synonymous with what Kestenberg calls "tension flow" (Kestenberg, 1965).

[c] As the items indicate here, a movement may be called "fast" or "rapid" for a number of reasons—e.g., it takes a short time relative to other movements, begins quickly as in a startle, accelerates, etc.

[d] See Hutchinson, 1970, pp. 357-359

[e] Actually this must involve a judgment based on complex phenomena such as the position of the one regarded as leading, the type of movement he makes, etc.

[f] The distinctions made in J, K, and L are not explicitly made by the movement notation systems, although many of them might be derived from an examination of a score. They are added here because of their importance in behavioral research. The terms in J are discussed by the author in another source (Bartenieff, Davis, and Paulay, 1972).

[g] Cf. "key signature" in Labanotation, which is an indication at the beginning of the score that such and such a position or detail of the movement is maintained or repeated throughout.

[h] A terminology of phrases of movement is virtually undeveloped.

As has been discussed, movement notations have to be very detailed and accurate descriptive systems because they are used for preservation and reconstruction. That is, a record must be complete enough that someone who has not seen the movement can "read" it from the score and reproduce the movement himself. Consequently, the notation systems have been extensively tested and in this sense are empirical tools that allow a high degree of replicability. The terminology is also of course rigorous and accurate. It must be stressed that although many of the terms listed in the glossary are common, everyday ones, in the notation systems they have precise, standardized meanings. While the glossary contains a number of general categories, many of the items are in fact "spelled out" and notated in greater detail than is indicated here. Suffice it to say that a trained notator could probably provide accurate, "operational" definitions of any movement or feature of movement that is of interest to a researcher.

Application of any of these systems to behavioral research doesn't necessarily mean having a notator sit and record every bit of the research data to obtain a movement "score." This would seem unnecessary for everything but the most detailed and complete analyses. Rather, they can be used flexibly with continual consideration as to what variables are most relevant, in what detail, and with what definition, What may not be clear from this presentation is that these are simply systematic descriptive tools that are very flexible. One can select, hone down, or elaborate on them according to one's interests and the dictates of the movement being studied. They essentially use general concepts, not arbitrary labels for specific movements.

The symbols and notation conventions may be more or less useful to a given researcher.[1] Probably if one seriously considered choosing one of the notations for research, the choice would depend greatly on what one wanted to quickly and systematically record. While all are accurate and logical, it seems that different systems display and record different aspects of the movement better than others. One could imagine a specialist in several systems consulting on a project and advising, "well, if you want to carefully record details of hand gestures, you might use Eshkol-Wachmann, but for the group relationships and formations, I suggest Labano-

---

[1] Irmgard Bartenieff has pointed out that notations have more than practical value; they bring out patterns and combinations that would be lost in a verbal description, and actually increase one's perception and understanding of the movement (personal communication, 1972).

tation," etc. Unfortunately, this is a fantasy, there are no experts versed in a number of notation systems.[2] In fact, there are very few specialists in movement analysis and notation who have experience in adapting their systems to the needs of a research project.

No further mention of the symbols and notations will be made here; rather, attention will be on the terminology and concepts of the systems. While only time will tell whether notations are useful in behavioral research, one can at present consider the value of the concepts and systematic terminology for clarifying existing research and for solving a number of problems in studying movement behavior.

[2] Ann Hutchinson is perhaps the closest to being such an "eclectic" notation expert (see Appendix II).

Chapter IV

APPLICATION OF THE MOVEMENT GLOSSARY TO THE LITERATURE

Experience in research has convinced this author that there is a need in the systematic study of movement behavior for more logical and rigorous ways of analyzing movement in its own terms. While I began with training in Laban's Effort-Shape Analysis and was continually surprised at the value of the system for behavioral research, it is clear that neither this system, nor probably any single system, is sufficient for any given research problem. Over the years, the more training I had in observation, the more variations, contrasts, and refinements I began to see and the more it became clear that there are patterns and features of movement that have yet to be defined. The questions repeatedly became: "How can that be described? What is the special nature of that movement? How could one define the difference between this pattern and that one? Doesn't such and such a system deal with that aspect of movement?" And gradually concepts from Labanotation in particular became absorbed into my vocabulary and my focus.

Again it was not a question here of adopting notation conventions, but of expanding the range of variables considered, of finding that some are more useful for certain problems than others. At this stage no system or lexicon could be complete enough. The systems presented in Chapter III were chosen because of their wide development, not with the assumption that they are individually or collectively the last word in movement analysis. The glossary is merely a tool for making certain analyses possible; it should be quite obsolete in a short time.

Another major influence on this thesis has been the study of the literature on body movement. Again I found myself continually asking: "What exactly is the author talking about? What movement is he looking at? What aspects of body motion is he concentrating on?" Often these questions cannot be answered because written language is either not precise enough or becomes a hopelessly convoluted string of adjectives and verbs describing what has occurred altogether in a split second. But in spite of the pitfalls in trying to reconstruct or extrapolate from the literature which aspects of movement the author is referring to, it can be done to a degree. And when it is done some interesting comparisons between studies can be made purely in terms of what movement variables or parameters are being used.

Chapter III is the result of formally analyzing the movement analysis systems to derive a glossary that I had come to believe through experience in research would be valuable. Chapter IV will be a formal analysis of the literature using this glossary.

I have chosen 17 contributions to movement literature that I consider to be important representatives from the areas reviewed in Chapter II. As shown in Table 3, these works range from studies of movement in relation to development to cultural differences in movement styles; they also include some of the "classic" and most frequently cited works in movement research. For practical reasons I have limited this analysis to one paper per author or to specific sections of an author's book. The works analyzed are, in effect, samples of how each author describes and analyzes movement.

The great variety in language and perspective that one finds in this literature is best illustrated by quoting the authors at their most explicit. Consider, for example, the following descriptions:

> Every neurotic is muscularly dystonic, and every cure is directly reflected in a change in muscular habitus. This is most readily observable in the compulsive character. His muscular rigidity is expressed in awkwardness, unrhythmical movements, particularly in the sexual act, a lack of mimetic expression, a typical rigidity of the facial musculature which often gives a mask-like impression. There is, typically, a deep line between nostril and corner of the mouth, and a certain rigid expression in the eyes resulting from a rigidity of the lid muscles. The musculature of the buttocks is always tense. (Reich, pp. 343-344)
>
> The two soldiers stood in parallel, legs akimbo with an intrafemoral index of 45 degrees. In unison, each raised his right upper arm

to about an 80-degree angle with his body and, with the lower arm at approximately a 100-degree angle, moved the arm in an anterior-posterior sweep with a double pivot at shoulder and elbow; the four fingers of the right hand were curled and the thumb was posteriorly hooked; the right palm faced the body. Their left arms were held closer to the body with an elbow bend of about 90 degrees. The left four fingers were curled and the thumb was partially hidden as it crooked into their respective belts. (Birdwhistell, pp. 176)

The experiments in which he scored among the highest 25% of subjects were: Speed of Estimating Distances to and from the Body with Hands, . . . Overestimation of Distance from Body with Legs, Fewness of Parallel Lines, Overestimation of Weights, Tapping Pressure, Pressure of Resting Hand, Grip or Finger Pressure on Stylus (1st place). He is first on the total Emphatic group factor, 7th on the Areal, and 13th on the Centrifugal . . . [these measurements] indicate correctly that his habits of movement are predominately firm, strong, forceful, emphatic, expansive, well spaced, and that his judgment is usually rapid. (Allport and Vernon, pp. 135-136)

Laughter is suppressed by the firm contraction of the orbicular muscles of the mouth, which prevents the great zygomatic and other muscles from drawing the lips backwards and upwards. The lower lip is also sometimes held by the teeth, and this gives a roguish expression to the face, as was observed with the blind and deaf Laura Bridgman. The great zygomatic muscle is sometimes variable in its course, and I have seen a young woman in whom the *depressores anguli oris* were brought into strong action in suppressing a smile; but this by no means gave to her countenance a melancholy expression, owing to the brightness of her eyes. (Darwin, p. 212)

His rhetorical gestures exhibited many of the tendencies found in the gestural behavior of ghetto Jews: confined sweep, "baton"- and "pointer"-type motions with the hand, "turtle-like" movements with the head, etc. Interrupted by a friend with an objection voiced in English, he performed a series of motions in which the quality of the "American" gesture was obvious. The radius became quite ample, the form straight and clear-cut, the stroke heavier, and the head stopped moving altogether. It was a distinct transition from one verb-gestural system to another. (Efron, p. 133)

Other postural configurations included holding her hands under her neck when fearful of being punished for masturbation; her right hand was lifted and her left hand held protectively over her head when she was angry with men. Her left hand was usually lifted when she was in a rage against her mother. Both arms were lifted when she felt hostile with both parents. Both arms were stretched backwards when longing for approval. (Deutsch, p. 201)

TABLE 3

WORKS CONSIDERED FOR GLOSSARY ANALYSIS

1. **Developmental Patterns.**

    Gesell, A. et al., *The First Five Years of Life,* 1940, pp. 30, 34-35, 41-42, 46-47, 52-53 (motor characteristics of children aged 1 through 5); pp. 67-107 (development of upright posture, locomotion, visual-prehensile coordination, laterality and directionality).

    Kestenberg, Judith S. et al., "Development of the Young Child as Expressed through Bodily Movement.I.", 1972.

2. **Emotion.**

    Darwin, Charles, *The Expression of the Emotions in Man and Animals,* 1872, pp. 147-150 (facial movements in weeping); pp. 176-177 (movements of grief); p. 213 (movements associated with love); pp. 238-239 (rage expressions); p. 254 (facial expressions of scorn); p. 264 (gestures of "helplessness").

3. **Personality and Psychopathology.**

    Allport, Gordon W. and Vernon, Philip E., *Studies in Expressive Movement,* 1933, pp. 134-151 ("psychomotor portraits" of 4 individual subjects).

    North, Marion, *Personality Assessment Through Movement,* 1972, pp. 19-21 (list of movement parameters used for individual movement styles), pp. 126-133 (movement-personality assessments of 3 children).

    Reich, Wilhelm, *Character Analysis,* 3rd ed., 1949, pp. 180-181 (physical manner of an "aristocratic" character), pp. 342-350 (in a section on "pleasure, anxiety, anger and muscular armor"), pp. 360-390 (emotional expression and the "segmental arrangement" of muscular armor).

    Lowen, Alexander, *Physical Dynamics of Character Structure,* 1958, pp. 173-177 (posture and tension patterns of the oral character); pp. 212-216 (musculature of the masochistic character); p. 242 (physical characteristics of an hysterical patient); pp. 372-376 (schizoid and schizophrenic features).

4. **Psychological Interpretation of Specific Actions.**

    Krout, Maurice H., "An Experimental Attempt to Produce Unconscious Manual Symbolic Movements", 1954, pp. 93-120.

Ekman, Paul and Friesen, Wallace V[a], "Nonverbal Behavior in Psychotherapy Research", in *Research in Psychotherapy, Vol. III,* ed. J. M. Shlien, 1968, pp. 179-216.

Deutsch, Felix, "Analysis of Postural Behavior", 1947, pp. 195-213.

Mahl, George F., "Gestures and Body Movements in Interviews", in *Research in Psychotherapy, Vol. III,* ed. J. M. Shlien, 1968, pp. 295-346.

5. Interaction and Communication.

Scheflen, Albert E., *The Stream and Structure of Communicational Behavior: Context Analysis of a Psychotherapy Session,* 1965, pp. 44-47 (diagrams of postural-kinesic intervals and alternations); pp. 66-70 (definitions of postural relationships); pp. 117-120 (the "program of postural progression" between co-therapists); pp. 141-159 (drawings and descriptions of specific "points" and "positions," communication units, and "quasi-courting behaviors").

Condon, William S., "Linguistic-Kinesic Research and Dance Therapy", 1968, pp. 21-42.

Kendon, Adam, "Some Relationships between Body Motion and Speech: An Analysis of an Example", in *Studies in Dyadic Communication,* ed. by Siegman and Pope, 1972, pp. 177-210.

Birdwhistell, Ray L., *Kinesics and Context,* 1970, pp. 19-23 (mother-infant interaction); pp. 121-125 and 239-248 (analysis of movement with speech); pp. 173-176 (interaction between hitchhikers and driver); pp. 283-285 (mother-son interaction on bus); p. 100 (American kinemes); pp. 206-207 ("body-set cross-referencing signals" of higher and lower status businessmen); pp. 208-211 (differences between "Bluegrass and Hill Kentuckians"); pp. 278-282 (walking styles).

6. Cultural Comparisons.

Efron, David, *Gesture and Environment,* 1941, pp. 43-78 (detailed analysis of movement patterns of first generation Jews); pp. 103-130 (table of differences between ghetto Jews and Italians and analysis of movement patterns of "assimilated" Jews and Italians).

Lomax, Alan; Bartenieff, Irmgard, and Paulay, Forrestine, "The Choreometric Coding Book", in *Folksong Style and Culture,* ed. A. Lomax, 1968, pp. 262-273.

---

[a] Ekman and Friesen's research covers many years and cannot be represented by one work. However, much of it involves examining consistency in the *judgment* of facial expression and so would not be appropriate for lexicon analysis. The example selected involved assessment of the movements of patients from film and would seem a good selection for this purpose.

If one were given a list that said "Darwin, biologist; Deutsch, psychoanalyst; Reich, psychoanalyst; Birdwhistell, linguistics-oriented anthropologist; Efron, anthropologist; Allport and Vernon, research psychologists," it wouldn't be hard to match correctly the authors with the quotes. The language they each use and the problems they focus on are clearly typical of their respective disciplines. However, one can still compare them in terms of what parameters of movement they are focusing on, irrespective of the conventions of their disciplines.

What can and will be done for the 17 references cited in Table 3 is a kind of semi-translation of these descriptions into the glossary terms. For example, in the Reich quotation to follow, terms from the glossary are put in brackets:

> Every neurotic is muscularly dystonic [disturbance in muscle tonus and tension], and every cure is directly reflected in a change in muscular habitus [constant or recurring features]. This is most readily observable in the compulsive character. His muscular rigidity [muscle tension, constant characteristic] is expressed in awkwardness, unrhythmical movements [see footnote 1 below], particularly in the sexual act, a lack of mimetic expression [presumably, few hand gestures], a typical rigidity of the facial musculature which often gives a mask-like impression [facial expression, muscle tension, holding]. There is, typically, a deep line between nostril and corner of the mouth, and a certain rigid expression in the eyes resulting from a rigidity of the lid muscles [again, muscle tension, holding]. The musculature of the buttocks is always tense [muscle tension, surface area; overall focus on moderate degree of detail of entire body].

To summarize then, Reich repeatedly attends to muscle tension and holding in any part or area of the body. He is particularly concerned with disturbance, in this case forms of "rigidity" and "awkwardness," and concentrates on features of expression that are chronic or persistent for the individual over time. This contrasts markedly with Birdwhistell's example:

> The two soldiers stood in parallel [same bilateral position], legs akimbo with an intrafemoral index of 45 degrees [range, thighs rotated outward]. In unison [group synchrony], each raised his right upper arm to about an 80-degree angle with his body and,

[1] Cf. "awkwardness" and "unrhythmical" movements—this could imply a number of features such as a lack of successiveness, or synchrony, or a predominance of holding in certain areas, angular transitions in the movement, etc. Because of their ambiguity, such words would not be translated. For a term or phrase to be assessed in glossary terms, it must be relatively straightforward and unambiguous.

[2] In some ways Birdwhistell's description of degrees of angles is similar to an Eshkol-Wachmann analysis of the range of the movement and limb angle geometrically defined. However, he does not usually indicate what planes the limb action occurs in or what types of figures are created in space, so his descriptions could not be readily translated into Eshkol-Wachmann terms.

with the lower arm at approximately a 100-degree angle [right-left distinctions, range[2]], moved the arm in an anterior-posterior sweep with a double pivot at shoulder and elbow [direction, rotation]; the four fingers of the right hand were curled and the thumb was posteriorly hooked [right-left distinction, position, NB focuses on any body part]; the right palm faced the body [surface area]; their left arms were held closer to the body with an elbow bend of about 90 degrees [again right-left distinction, range, position]. The left four fingers were curled and the thumb was partially hidden as it crooked into their respective belts [self-touch, group synchrony; overall this is a "micro" unit analysis with a relatively high degree of body part detail].

To complete this illustration of how specific works may be analyzed according to the terms of the glossary, I will conclude with a "translation" of the first sentences in the remaining quotes:

> The experiments in which he scored among the highest 25% of subjects were: Speed of Estimating Distances to and from the Body with Hands [duration, range, in-out dimension, upper limbs] . . .
>
> (Allport and Vernon)

> Laughter is suppressed by the firm contraction of the orbicular muscles of the mouth [muscle tension, facial movement], which prevents the great zygomatic and other muscles from drawing the lips backwards and upwards [first phrases plus this indicates downward direction, holding].
>
> (Darwin)

> His rhetorical gestures exhibited many of the tendencies found in the gestural behavior of ghetto Jews [recurring characteristics]: confined sweep [range], "baton"- and "pointer"-type motions with hand [spatial path, upper limbs], "turtle-like" movements with the head, etc. [apparently head movements "shrinking" inward].
>
> (Efron)

> Other postural configurations included holding her hands under her neck when fearful of being punished for masturbation [upper limbs, position]; her right hand was lifted and her left hand held protectively over her head when she was angry with men [upper limbs, right-left distinctions, positions].
>
> (Deutsch)

Scanning these samples it can be seen that they differ greatly in terms of which body parts are attended to, the "sizes" of the units considered, and the aspects of movement focused on, from chronic muscle tension of the whole body to minute head turns occurring in a split second. The 17 works previously listed, of which these are samples, were examined in the way illustrated above. If one considers what movement parameters each is *primarily* dealing with, a chart can be obtained that allows one to easily compare and contrast them. Three considerations figured in the evaluation of each work in this way: first, is the parameter a primary one for the work (i.e., repeatedly mentioned as opposed to rarely referred to); secondly, is the parameter actually similar to a particular glossary term or heading (i.e., can it be thus classified without seriously distorting the author's meaning); and third, are there special ways in which the parameter is defined that are unique to the particular study? For example, Lowen talks repeatedly about what could be classified as Body Attitude or Posture, but in a very different way from the way in which Lomax, Bartenieff, and Paulay define body attitude in their research. This third consideration will be discussed later; the following table (Table 4) was developed from an analysis of the 17 works according to which terms and concepts they primarily deal with. Again, the reader is referred to Appendix I for a description of the works.

While the analysis presented in Table 4 may seem too detailed at first glance, it is clear at second glance that, in fact, it is in many ways too gross. For example, one might legitimately state that every study considers movements of the upper limbs and that this has general significance. But with this item, as with almost every term of the lexicon, a closer look shows that each researcher defines or delimits the term in a slightly different way. Only a few major examples of this can be dealt with here. Perhaps if this study proves useful, someone such as a trained movement analyst may do a more intensive analysis than is here appropriate.

From a close look at a category such as "Body Part" it can be seen that the studies differ in degree of detail and inclusiveness. They also may differ greatly in *how* they define a given parameter. For example, "Body Attitude" in choremetrics (Lomax et al.) is defined (a) according to whether the trunk is moved as a unit or is divided through twists or undulations and (b) according to the predominant spatial tendencies of the attitude (axis held, vertical held, frontal plane, vertical-diagonal stress, etc.) (Lomax et al., 1968, pp. 266-267). "Posture" as analyzed by Lowen is a complex configuration of contractions, rigidities, and inert areas described in terms of what muscle groups are held, the overall alignment of head, limbs, and trunk, and the way the weight is placed. In other words, not only is Lowen's description more detailed, but it includes different variables (i.e., muscle tension, weight placement, localized configurations) than those of Lomax, Bartenieff, and Paulay.

To cite another contrast. Some studies analyze facial movement in terms of the degree of articulation and/or moment-to-moment change in direction (Birdwhistell, Condon). Others describe it in terms of "expressions"—i.e., complex configurations usually given labels such as "smiles," "frown," "looks angry," etc. (Kestenberg, Lowen, Reich). Interestingly, Darwin, who devotes most of his attention to facial expressions, does a mixture of both: he combines minute analysis of what each area "does" with common terms for the overall expression.

It is interesting to compare the studies with respect to the degree to which they focus on states or static positions vs. movement as a continuous process of change. For example, "muscle tension" is frequently referred to, but some writers appear to observe fixed states of contraction or hypertension (Lowen) while others observe continuous fluctuations and "rhythms" of tension change (Kestenberg, Reich). Still others may refer to "momentary" states of tension or flaccidity (Birdwhistell). The same can be said for what is labelled here the "in-out" dimension. For some writers inward and outward refer primarily to held positions (Scheflen, Deutsch, Lowen). For others, the reference is to a continual dynamic emphasis or fluctuating pattern (Allport and Vernon, Kestenberg). Close examination shows that some writers concentrate far more on positions or static phenomena than do others. Also, the language that is used and the means of recording or measuring conveys more or less mobility. Some writers can describe what is obviously a movement in terms so static that it sounds like a concrete thing or a fixed position.

"Surface area" is cited when the term is used in either of two ways. Scheflen is listed under this item because he talks about the way the patient "exposes" certain areas of the body such as the thigh or palm. Darwin, Lowen, and Reich are listed here because they attend so closely to changes in skin tonus and color and in the tension of various surfaces. Birdwhistell may focus on both surface as "exposed" and surface as subtly changed. Not listed here are those who indirectly refer to body surfaces when they describe touch patterns (e.g., "touches cheek").

Perhaps one of the most significant differences in how these studies delimit a given parameter is in terms of the relative constancy and context specificity with which the parameter is used. For example, Scheflen may describe position in psychotherapy in terms not that different from those of Deutsch, but Scheflen is referring to positions that continually change within the session and he is concerned with the sequence of changes itself. Deutsch, however, refers to positions that he observed to recur over periods of months or even years: he summarizes the positions

TABLE 4

MOVEMENT ANALYSIS OF LITERATURE EXAMPLES

Movement Category[a]	Gesell et al.	Kestenberg et al.	Darwin	Allport & Vernon	North
I. Maintained Aspects					
A. Body Attitude or Posture	X				X
B. Position					
C. Hold			X		X
II. Mobile Aspects					
A. Body Parts					
1. Entire body					
a. high detail					
b. medium detail					
c. low detail	X	X			X
2. Selective					
a. head			X		
b. upper limbs			X	X	
c. lower limbs				X	
d. trunk					
e. facial expression[b]			X		

[a] Definitions of the movement categories can be found in the glossary of pages 37 to 42. See Table 3 of this chapter for the exact literature sources; here they are indicated by author only.

[b] Birdwhistell, Condon, and Lomax note movement of the face in terms of parts articulated; Lowen, Kestenberg, and Reich attend to the face as in "facial expression." They all make special note of facial movement but are not listed here because they are listed as researchers who focus on all parts of the body.

REFERENCES

Reich	Lowen	Krout	Ekman & Freisen	Deutsch	Mahl	Scheflen	Condon	Kendon	Birdwhistell	Efron	Lomax, Bartenieff, Paulay
X	X				X				X		X
		X		X	X	X		X	X		
X	X			X			X	X	X		
							X		X		
X	X					X		X			X
				X	X					X	
		X	X	X	X					X	
			X	X	X						

Movement Category

	Gesell et al.	Kestenberg et al.	Darwin	Allport & Vernon	North
3. Visual behavior					
a. mutual eye contact or focus on other					
b. focus patterns per se	X		X		
4. Surface areas			X		
5. Types of relationships					
a. successive-simultaneous					X
b. unilateral-bilateral	X				X
c. synchronous					
d. right-left distinctions	X				
e. initiating or leading part					X
f. active-passive					
6. Gesture-posture					
B. Spatial Aspects					
1. Areas of space					X
2. In-out dimension		X	X	X	X
3. Direction	X	X	X		X
4. Planal stress	X	X			
5. Plane movement					X
6. Types of path					X

REFERENCES

Reich	Lowen	Krout	Ekman & Freisen	Deutsch	Mahl	Scheflen	Condon	Kendon	Birdwhistell	Efron	Lomax, Bartenieff, Paulay
						X			X		
X	X					X			X		
											X
					X		X			X	
							X				
			X	X				X	X		
											X
								X	X		
X	X		X		X						
X			X	X	X		X	X	X		
									X	X	
										X	
									X		

TABLE 4 continued

Movement Category	Gesell et al.	Kestenberg et al.	Darwin	Allport & Vernon	North
7. Figures in space					X
8. Spatial transitions					
9. Size or range		X		X	X
10. Qualitative					
a. vague-clear	X				X
b. direct-sinuous					X
C. Kinesiological Terms					
1. Flexion-extension	X				
2. Rotation	X				
D. Tension-Related Terms					
1. Relaxed, tense			X	X	
2. Effort flow		X			X
E. Weight-Related Terms					
1. Support	X				X
2. Center of weight		X			X
3. Weight shifts	X	X			X
4. Qualitative terms					
a. heavy					X
b. forceful			X	X	X
c. light					X
d. weak, tentative					X
e. giving into gravity		X	X		

REFERENCES

Reich	Lowen	Krout	Ekman & Freisen	Deutsch	Mahl	Scheflen	Condon	Kendon	Birdwhistell	Efron	Lomax, Bartenieff, Paulay
											X
										X	X
					X				X	X	
											X
										X	
							X	X	X		
			X		X		X	X	X		
X	X				X				X		
X											X
	X										
	X										
									X		
X	X				X				X	X	X
		X									

TABLE 4 continued

Movement Category	Gesell et al.	Kestenberg et al.	Darwin	Allport & Vernon	North
F. Time-Related Terms					
1. Duration				X	
2. Tempo				X	
3. Acceleration-deceleration	X				
4. Qualitative terms					
a. sudden					X
b. sustained					X
5. Rhythmic synchrony					
G. Touch Patterns in Relation to:					
1. Self					
2. Other		X	X		
3. Object	X				
H. Locomotion					
1. Turns	X				
2. Jumps	X				
3. Steps	X				
4. "Floor pattern"					
5. Types of walk	X	X		X	
I. Group Relationships					
1. Group formations					

REFERENCES

Reich	Lowen	Krout	Ekman & Freisen	Deutsch	Mahl	Scheflen	Condon	Kendon	Birdwhistell	Efron	Lomax, Bartenieff, Paulay
			X			X			X		
											X
										X	X
					X					X	
					X						
											X
		X	X	X	X					X	
						X			X	X	
					X	X				X	
									X		
X									X		
					X						

TABLE 4 continued

Movement Category	Gesell et al.	Kestenberg et al.	Darwin	Allport & Vernon	North
2. Types of relationships					
a. orientation					
b. toward-away		X			
c. proximity					
d. symmetry					
e. opposition					
f. synchrony		X			
g. common focal point					
h. succession					
i. leading, following					X
j. "floor plans"					
J. Pattern Features					
1. Recurring characteristics				X	X
2. Types of phrases		X			X
3. Types of motifs					
4. Composition					
K. Unit Length					
1. 1/48 - 2 seconds		X			
2. 2 - 15 seconds		X	X		X
3. 15 seconds - 2 minutes					
4. 2 - 30 minutes					
L. Amount or Frequency					

REFERENCES

Reich	Lowen	Krout	Ekman & Freisen	Deutsch	Mahl	Scheflen	Condon	Kendon	Birdwhistell	Efron	Lomax, Bartenieff, Paulay
						X			X		
						X		X	X		
						X				X	
						X					
						X	X		X		
						X					
X	X			X	X				X	X	X
										X	
										X	
					X						
							X		X		
	X	X						X		X	
			X		X			X			
			X	X	X						
	X	X	X	X						X	

63

in relation to the themes of the patient but rarely in terms of the sequence of events in an actual session.[3] To give another, more extreme, example, North observes the predominant movement characteristics of a child that recur over a period of time and that are presumably present in different contexts. In contrast, Birdwhistell's analysis of the soldiers' thumbing a ride is highly detailed and context specific, a blow-by-blow description of the actual behaviors of that context. Presumably, the analysis is generalizable only to other similar contexts and the soldiers may move quite differently in other contexts.

As can be seen in Table 4, Birdwhistell refers to many different aspects of movement; but on close examination one sees a rather clear "clustering" of certain variables when he addresses himself to particular areas. Thus, when he presents specific, "blow by blow" examples either of interaction or speech-motion relationships, he primarily notes direction, pauses, body parts and surfaces, synchrony, angles created by limbs, touch patterns, and what is done in "micro" detail. However, when he focuses on contrasts between different groups, or when the observations appear primarily to discriminate and identify cultural or social role motion differences, he may use additional parameters such as degree of muscle tension and tonus, postural and position characteristics, duration, and range. (Additional distinctions such as bilateral-unilateral, mirror behavior, "production rate," and integrated vs. fragmented movement are cited by him as useful (Birdwhistell, 1970, pp. 216-218), but rarely appear in specific examples of kinesic analysis.) It must be stated that Birdwhistell considers all of his observations to have communicational significance and so such a division is a false one in kinesic theory. Nevertheless, in a purely descriptive sense, it appears to bear out in his examples. The cluster of variables used for interaction sequences or speech-motion patterns (to be referred to later as Birdwhistell$_1$) differs in certain ways from the cluster of variables used when the stress is on identifying movement features of a specific role or group (to be referred to later as Birdwhistell$_2$).

There are great variations in the types of records or "end-products" that the studies present. Some researchers, such as Birdwhistell, Condon, Scheflen, and Kendon, present detailed, "blow by blow" records of the behaviors as they occur over time, although they may differ in the degree of detail and the parameters attended to. Such studies are rather like the "scores" of recordings of the movement notation systems. Other re-

---

[3]This is true for Deutsch's early articles such as the one used in this analysis. Later, he did consecutive analyses of actual sessions (Deutsch, 1966).

searchers present inventories or profiles—lists of features observed to be characteristic of the movement under study (Lomax, Bartenieff, and Paulay; North; Efron) or tallies of what movements most frequently occurred (Ekman, Krout, Mahl). Still others present anecdotal descriptions of the subject's transitory movements (Mahl, Deutsch), general expressions (Darwin, Reich, Lowen), or general trends of development (Gesell, Kestenberg), using anatomical or kinesiological terms or commonly understood action language. Only two of the studies analyzed here report scores from experimental measurement of subjects' movements using apparatus (Allport and Vernon, and Gesell). (Most studies selected for this analysis are based on direct observation, of course.)

One could also consider the degree to which the studies focus on action, on *what* the subject is doing (e.g., lit cigarette, crossed legs, rubbed his nose, placed one block on another, etc.). With reports that primarily involve descriptions of actions (e.g., Scheflen, Ekman, Deutsch, and Krout), one has to make inferences as to the character of the movement itself. However, no effort has been made here to classify the actions or infer what their "movement character" might be beyond what is clear from the author's descriptions. It is noteworthy that those who concentrate on what is done often concentrate on position as well; they are perhaps less movement oriented.

Sometimes, as with Reich or Darwin, a great many adjectives such as "awkward," "refined," and "mechanical" are used to describe movements. Such adjectives can be highly evocative of movement patterns and qualities, but it is difficult to discern what exactly are their movement referents; therefore, in the analysis for Table 4, adjectives were not translated into the glossary terms in this way. A particular term or feature was attributed to a study if it was described so clearly that it appeared to be virtually synonymous with the glossary term. One of the advantages of a systematic analysis of a movement in its own terms is that one can define why the movement appears awkward, refined, integrated, etc. if the descriptive system is dynamic enough. Suffice it to say here that it seems that when adjectives such as graceful, agitated, delicate, etc. are used, the observer is responding at least in part to the intensity or dynamic quality of the movement (its emphasis, tempo, fluency, etc.).

I will conclude with a note about terms used in various studies that are not included in the glossary. Some studies use well-established terms, such as the extensive anatomical descriptions of Darwin, Reich, and Lowen. Of course an analysis of localized muscle action is not done very well from direct observation of the person moving; hence Darwin relied on anatomical drawings, and Reich and Lowen seem to utilize their medical training when they may palpate an area or observe the fairly gross activity of muscle groups. At the level of what can be directly observed in movement, however, there are some observations not categorized in Table 4 that seem unique. For example, Condon suggests that one important relationship between people in face-to-face communication has to do with the angles and geometric forms their bodies make with respect to each other, "planar fields or line vectors shared by speaker and listener" (Condon, p. 37).

Lomax et al. and Reich describe patterns in which the movement flows from the center of the trunk outward, although they define the movement differently (Lomax, p. 273; Reich, p. 388). Reich describes specific "rings" of "muscle armoring" arranged segmentally from head to legs. Darwin has a seemingly unique way of describing the gradations or gradual changes of a facial expression (Darwin, p. 208). Marion North refers to "counter-directions" in the body and to "chordic" features of movement (North, p. 20). Doubtless there are more special terms and nuances of observation in the studies than are cited here. Some studies seem untapped in terms of their usefulness for research as are a number of the rarely used terms of the lexicon (e.g., "floor pattern," "initiating").

But even after all the terms are considered, one has to agree with Reich that movement is a phenomenon with a language of its own that words do not do justice to (Reich, pp. 360-362). One has a feeling that there are phenomena yet to be described and visual and kinesthetic perceptions that will always defy description.

Chapter V

CORRELATIONS BETWEEN SPECIFIC MOVEMENT PATTERNS AND BEHAVIORAL PHENOMENA

CONSISTENCIES IN PARAMETER SELECTION

It is appropriate at this point to examine the relationships between what movement parameters a researcher uses and what he is interested in studying. As has been said before, very little attention is paid in the literature to the properties of the movement dimension itself and its systematic description. One rarely finds discussions of why a researcher focused on positions over movements or on direction over tempo. If there are explanations of the terminology used, they usually deal with theoretical assumptions such as that self-directed hand activity is "self-communication" and therefore useful for a study of unconscious symbolic processes, as opposed to the gesticulations that accompany speech (Krout, 1954a, p. 94). Researchers have rarely discussed the nature of movement itself as somehow playing a part in their selection of parameters.

However, a close look at Table 4 and the movement variables researchers use for a given problem yields some interesting data. The most obvious observation is that those who are concerned with interpersonal processes pick "group relationship" items in movement (see p. 60). Recalling that historically there is a shift in the literature from a personality and intrapsychic orientation to a focus on communication and small-group interaction, it is no surprise that the communication researchers (e.g., Birdwhistell, Condon, Scheflen) provide the bulk of the entries under group movement parameters: group formation, orientation, synchrony, etc. Reich, in contrast, is not directly interested in group interaction; he says nothing about the relationship between his movements and those of the patient. He is interested in character, so he uses parameters that describe the individual mover, and he focuses on "chronic," persistent characteristics. From this perspective, the most purely "interactional" of the researchers—i.e., the one who concentrates most on group-level variables, and least on individual differences or cultural styles per se—is Scheflen. Scheflen examines the group formation, positions, and proximity of movers vis a vis each other, movements toward and away, symmetrical and synchronous activity, succession of actions, and what is termed in the lexicon the overall composition.

It is possible to read the entries in Table 4 for a single work and deduce something of the author's discipline, orientation, and subject of interest. Rather like putting the cart before the horse, it is an exercise which makes a point—the variables and terms the researcher picks (however consciously or unconsciously) reflect what he is studying and how. Consider, for example, someone who focuses on

> the body and facial expression in a fairly gross way; the areas of space, directions, and planes predominantly moved in; very fine details and phases of "growing" and "shrinking" in space and fluctuations in muscle tension; relationship to center of weight, weight shift, and giving into gravity; types of walk and patterns of touching others and objects; and finally, patterns of synchrony and moving toward or away from another.

Would it be surprising that this is someone studying the movement patterns of babies and young children, stages of development, and patterns of intimate relatedness between mother and infant as reflected in movement? (See Kestenberg entries in Table 4.) To elaborate on this line of thinking, consider another example in which the primary focus is on

> posture, visual behavior, the entire body in a gross way; laterality and coordination of body parts; primary directions and spatial planes; patterns of flexion, extension, and rotation; the degree of clarity of the movement; patterns of weight support, weight shifts, turns, jumps, steps, and types of walk; acceleration-deceleration features; and finally relationship to objects.

This could well be an appropriate list of parameters for someone studying infant motor development in terms of locomotion, posture, and visual-prehensile stages (see Gesell entries of Table 4). Kestenberg and Gesell are the two examples of infant research in the list of 17 studies. It is notable that they share some items in common. They see that the baby goes through stages in which one plane is predominant and they describe the child's growing control over balance, weight shift, prehension of objects. The progression from total body reaction and unclear projection in space to movement refined in body articulation, space, and pacing is also described by both. But they differ in emphasis and this is reflected in what they focus on in movement. Gesell stresses coordination and mastery of locomotion and prehension. Kestenberg attends to subtle fluctuations in tension and "in-outedness" observed in all activity. She is concerned with "drive discharge," affect development, and stages of symbiosis with and differentiation from the mother. The differences between Kestenberg and Gesell are suggested in a gross way by the parameters they use; a closer look at how they define these general parameters would reveal even more clearly their different perspectives.

To take another example, if one wanted to study the relationship between body movements and speech structure (not its content), what would be the likely movement variables to consider? If the focus is on how speech inflection, emphasis, and structure is coordinated with movements, the choice of variables would first depend on the degree of detail and the "size" or length of the variable. If one attends to minute units such as phonemes, events which can occur in a fraction of a second, then one would have to attend to perceptible changes in movement that are of comparable length and refinement. The most readily perceptible variables for this are the subtle changes in direction and fine articulation and coordination of eye, face, head, and hand so clear in slow motion film. Birdwhistell seems to be studying this when he presents his micro-analyses of linguistic-kinesic correlations (Birdwhistell, 1970, pp. 136-137). And Kendon uses the same parameters (direction and body part, sequence and combination) at a grosser or "larger" level when he examines the correlation between certain "larger" linguistic units (e.g., "prosodic phrases") and movements (Kendon, 1972). In other words, if one is interested in correlations between speech *structure* (not content, "meaning," or paralinguistic phenomena) and movement, then one would do well to focus on movement "structure,"—i.e., on the combinations and sequences of direction and body part change—at the appropriate level of detail.

ANALYSIS OF MOVEMENT STYLE

Finally an example showing what entries under one item of the glossary "tell" about the researches. There are nine works listed under "recurring characteristics" (see entry II. J. 1. Table 4). This item refers to constant or recurring characteristics or stylistic features—i.e., a position or detail of the movement which is maintained or repeated throughout the behavior observed. Allport and Vernon are included here because the motor patterns they experimentally measured were found to have repeat reliability and persisted across task, body part doing the task, etc. Mahl is cited because he summarizes the actions observed during a psychotherapy session, presumably considering them fairly set characteristics of the patient. Deutsch, Lowen, and Reich are included here because they also note the style or repertoire of the patient's movements which persist over time. Birdwhistell, Efron, and Lomax et al. are included because they note patterns that are prevalent movement characteristics of different regional or cultural groups (Birdwhistell, 1970, pp. 208-210). North is cited because she also attends to movement style over time—i.e., not moment-to-moment actions specific to a context or a single interaction, but movements characteristic of the individual child across contexts.

So all of these researchers are in some way concerned with "style." They differ in that they may use different measures or variables to delineate the style and also in the "level" of discrimination they are making. Allport and Vernon, North, Deutsch, Reich, Mahl, and Lowen are variously analyzing individual style. Efron and Birdwhistell are describing national or regional differences in kinesic patterns. And Lomax et al. are defining styles of large cultural groups that cut across national lines.

What comes through in such an analysis is that there are really very few works that are in direct contradiction or irreconcilable conflict with each other at the descriptive level. When one considers what parameters they attend to and how, it is clear that some studies are, figuratively speaking, talking about oranges, some about pears, and some about cherries. So that from a purely objective, methodological and definitional standpoint, one researcher's findings cannot be used to call into question another's results.

This has theoretical implications. There is something of a controversy now as to whether movement is essentially *inter*personally or *intra*personally significant. It is in a way a debate as to whether a given movement reflects one's culture and role in a group or one's personality make-up or emotional state. Without getting into complex theoretical discussions as to personality vs. cultural determinants of movement, a strong case can be made that it depends on how one analyzes the movement. The studies reviewed here appear to be saying (more or less explicitly) that if one wants to discriminate one group from another, look at variables A, B, and C in such and such a way, but if one wants to discriminate individual differences in movement, then attend to variables X, Y, and Z in a fairly

TABLE 5

MOVEMENT PARAMETERS USED TO DIFFERENTIATE DIFFERENT LEVELS OF ANALYSIS

Level	Parameters
LARGE CULTURAL DIVISIONS	Type of body attitude; spatial transition and degree of complexity as defined by Lomax, Bartenieff, and Paulay (1968)
SINGLE CULTURE OR NATIONALITY	Radius, limb articulation, spatial path, laterality, right-left alternation, plane stress, tempo, and touch patterns as measured by Efron (1941, pp. 103-105)
SOCIAL — Class	Amount or frequency of gesticulating (Efron, 1941, pp. 124-125)
SOCIAL — Status	Who initiates touch (Henley, 1970); postural orientation as defined by Mehrabian (1969)
ROLE — Sex	Amount of eye contact (Exline et al., 1965); "tertiary sexual characteristics" such as pelvic angle (Birdwhistell, p. 42-44)
Developmental Stages	Ease of reversing direction (Singleton, 1954); articulation of body parts and types of prehension as defined by Gesell et al. (1940)
INDIVIDUAL DIFFERENCES	Characteristic repertoire of actions (Mahl, 1968); characteristic patterns of effort qualities and effort flow variations as analyzed by North (1972); individual patterns in motor speed, pressure, range, and "centrifugality" (Allport and Vernon, 1933); configurations of muscle tension in head, trunk, and limbs (Reich, 1949; Lowen, 1958)
TOTAL "STYLE"	

detailed way. In both cases the focus is on what is predominant or characteristic for the individual or for the group-as-a-whole.

Table 5 analyzes the studies of stylistic differences in such a way as to demonstrate how they complement each other. It shows that one can arrange the studies in a hierarchical way in order to show how they discriminate differences between one individual or group and another—from individual differences to social role behaviors to cultural characteristics.[2] That is, because each uses different movement parameters—ones which complement each other when considered collectively—they can be arranged hierarchically to give a view of overall movement style. Not only do they complement each other, but taken as preliminary data, they suggest that it is possible to obtain a wide range of information from any given movement. As will be seen, those studies making "style" differentiations (i.e., those cited in Table 4 under "recurring characteristics") are listed in Table 5 according to the level of analysis they make. Some other references have been added to fill out the table.

If the mode of analysis illustrated in Table 5 is viable, then it may be possible someday to observe someone's movements over a limited period of time and, by noting a wide range of movement characteristics in varying degrees of detail such as Table 5 suggests, learn something about where the person is from, the person's age, social status, sex, and class, as well as certain individual characteristics presumably related to his personality make-up. There is some indication from Birdwhistell that it also may be possible to determine the region of the country the person comes from, his "movement dialect," so to speak (Birdwhistell, 1970, pp. 208-210). In addition, there is research on how one might analyze a subject's mental status (Davis, 1970; Wolff, 1945), mood (Clynes, 1970; Darwin, 1872), and perhaps even his intelligence from movement (North, 1972). What is most important here is the possibility demonstrated by Table 5 that none of the researchers contradict each other on the movement level. An individual may be seen to possess all of these movement characteristics because movement is itself so complex and multi-faceted. Table 5

---

[1] Of course one could still raise questions about some studies as to whether the movement discriminations made between individual subjects are in fact mixed with cultural style features. For example, Allport and Vernon describe one subject's movement and make note that he is "unmistakably Italian in type" (Allport and Vernon, 1933, p. 137), but they disregard the cultural aspects of their other subjects as if these were not salient.

[2] Birdwhistell appears to be doing a similar kind of analysis (Birdwhistell, 1970, p. 206) when he discusses "body-set cross-referencing signals," presenting examples of behaviors discriminating age, status, territoriality, etc. However, it is difficult to determine what the movement referents are.

has been arranged in such a way that one's overall movement "style" can be seen as a gestalt of all of these levels. Moreover, these analyses of style or population characteristics do not necessarily contradict analyses of the movement the individual makes in interaction or of the group's nonverbal "program." As has been pointed out, the group movement variables are distinctly different (see Table 4, p. 60).

To recapitulate this chapter, those who, like Scheflen and Condon, primarily study interpersonal processes tend to select group relationship terms, direction terms, and body part terms and to define them with more or less detail depending on how exhaustive or refined their analysis of the interaction event. Those studying national differences pick fairly complex measures—area of space, tempo, proximity patterns, etc. (cf. Efron, Hall)—and define them with enough detail to capture what is characteristic of a given group in various settings in contrast to other groups. Those studying large cultural differences and comparing groups around the world pick variables such as predominant body attitude (Lomax et al.) or characteristic sitting and standing postures (Hewes) rather "grossly" defined. They mainly select behaviors that not only everyone must display but that are also fundamental for survival and for the organization of any activity. In other words, they are not variables like speaking gestures, which might be highly variable in form and use from region to region, and which are not necessary to survival.

Those who study individual differences use a wide range of variables from muscle tension configurations of one's posture (Reich, Lowen) to subtle differences in speed, fluency, and rhythmic phrasing (Kestenberg, North), but with stress on distinguishing characteristic movement patterns of one individual from those of another. The distinctions may be as subtle and refined as they are for group interaction, but they are made according to what is "chronic," constant, or repeated for the individual.

Finally, it may sometimes happen that someone studying cultural differences picks the same general parameter as someone studying individual differences. For example, Efron talks about predominant planes used and the rhythmic features of the movements of Italians vs. Jews (Efron, 1942), and North also notes predominant spatial tendencies and rhythmic patterns (North, 1970) in individual English children. There can be overlap here or confusion of levels, as in the example of Allport and Vernon's Italian subject. Nevertheless, close examination would indicate that Efron and North are delimiting the parameters somewhat differently. For example, more refined discriminations are usually made in studies of individual style.

One of the most interesting questions is: How do the various levels relate and how do cultural and individual style characteristics mesh with interaction programs? While this may seem too ambitious a question, it would appear possible to approach an answer through movement research, at least in a sketchy way. This is so because movement is visible, objectively describable, and, according to the research, reflective of a wide range of behavioral phenomena.

Chapter VI

THE QUESTION OF INTRINSIC SIGNIFICANCE

There seems to be method in the selection of movement variables that researchers make for a given study in spite of the great differences in their disciplines and/or orientations. How can one explain the trend towards using certain movement parameters for certain problems, parameters that by their nature or particular properties appear to have some relationship to the behavioral phenomena they are associated with? As can be seen in Table 4, the "group movement" variables are almost exclusively used by communication researchers (see p. 60), while variables having to do with muscle tension and weight, for example, are primarily utilized by those focusing on emotion or personality dynamics (see p. 58). One begins to feel that certain movement parameters, when defined in certain ways, "yield" information more readily about certain behavioral processes than others.

It is a central thesis of this dissertation that however diverse the studies are in approach and discipline, there are some shared assumptions as to the nature of movement. In Chapter V this notion was supported by observing that there is an underlying reasonableness in the selection of parameters for a given problem and in their definition. This line of thinking will now be extended to an examination of the relationship between movement observations and what they are associated with —i.e., I will attempt to support the idea that there is a fundamental relationship between the character of a movement and its significance.

"Significance" will be very broadly defined here: whatever psychological or social phenomena a particular movement pattern or characteristic is associated with by the researcher will be considered an interpretation as to its significance. That is, for purposes of theoretical discussion, I will take the various research results at face value irrespective of how rigorous the research and accurate the findings. In this sense, then, one is dealing with a wide range of associations such as:

> (1) "this movement (feature, pattern) was interpreted (by the interviewer, naive observer, movement analyst) to mean..."
> (2) "it was found that every time this movement occurred the subject was talking about such and such"
> (3) "this kind of movement was found in members X of culture Y in social context Z"

In other words, "significance" is defined here as that which the movement is associated with.

It may be noted that no distinction is made here between whether a movement is "communicative" or not, perceived and responded to by others, or part of a communication system. Determining whether a movement has communicative significance or function would itself appear to be a major issue. Again, "significance" is used here more broadly to refer to all associations between movements and behavioral phenomena, whether they are determined from (1) observer judgment, (2) research analysis of isolated factors in relation to independent measures, (3) Scheflen's context analysis, (4) correlational studies, or (5) clinical interpretation.

Thus, I will be examining the relationships between movement patterns and their significances across studies that vary greatly in methodology, experimental rigor, and goals. This is done with the assumption that these studies are important works that have been and/or are influencing research in movement and that their results may be compared at least for purposes of exploring certain theoretical issues regarding significance.

THREE TYPES OF RELATIONSHIPS BETWEEN A MOVEMENT AND ITS SIGNIFICANCE

Ekman and Friesen define three possible relationships between an act and what it signifies: "arbitrary" (and extrinsic), "iconic" (and extrinsic), and "intrinsic" (Ekman and Friesen, 1969, p. 60). They distinguish between acts that bear "no visual resemblance to what they signify" (arbitrary), those that "look in some way like what" they signify but the resemblance is somehow extrinsic (iconic), and those that not only resemble their significance but *are* at least in part the significant (intrinsic) (Ekman and Friesen, 1969, p. 60). They give as an example of the arbitrary case, opening and closing of the raised hand in greeting—i.e., there is no apparent resemblance between the act and what it signifies. They give as an example of "intrinsic," hitting someone during a conversation. It doesn't signify aggression; rather, it *is* a kind of aggression (Ekman and Friesen, 1969, p. 60). Their examples of "intrinsic" suggest that they are using this term in a narrow way to refer to "literal" actions or derivatives of actions.

In this dissertation these three terms will be somewhat differently defined. "Arbitrary" will refer here to relationships between a movement and its significance which are in every way "external" and without resemblance or apparent connection. For example, if one found that making a zig-zag motion of the hand with the thumb up always occurred during greetings, one would be hard pressed to see any apparent relationship between the form, rhythms, or "content" of the action and that with which it appears associated. The second term, "iconic," will be used here to refer to movements that have a perceptible resemblance to that which they are related to, but the resemblance is presumed to be purely extrinsic, like the road sign that has a curved arrow to signify a curve in the road. The resemblance is clear, but the relationship stops there. "Intrinsic" will be used more broadly than is done by Ekman and Friesen to refer to resemblances between a movement and its significance that are assumed to reflect an intimate connection, as is implied in the dictionary definition of the term. The dictionary defines "intrinsic" as "belonging to a thing by its very nature" (Random House, 1966); and Roget's Thesaurus offers synonyms for "intrinsic" such as "fundamental," "inherent," "essential," and "indigenous." That is, in the intrinsic case it is assumed here that the resemblances are resemblances because the movement is a part of, reflection, or essential element of the processes or behavioral phenomena with which it is associated.

In order to point out resemblances between a movement pattern and its significance(s), one may have to attend to rather abstract details or qualities of the movement. For example, Ekman and Friesen call raising the hand and opening and closing it in greeting, arbitrary. But if one considers the character of the movement—e.g., "open-closedness," "verticality," or "hand shown" or whatever—then there may be a perceptible relationship. The question often becomes one of how good the description is, because one cannot posit such resemblances if the movement isn't sufficiently described. Roughly speaking, one may see two types of iconic or intrinsic resemblance: (1) parallels between formal or qualitative aspects of the movement and its significance and (2) correspondences between the "content," or what action is done, and the significance. In the first case there may be resemblances with the rhythm, spatial pattern, organization, etc. of the movement—e.g., forceful, expansive actions correlated with an aggressive character trait, or a series of quick shakes of the hand to mean "hurry up." In the second case the resemblance is between *what* is done and what is meant—e.g., making a fist may be a derivative of a total action pattern of fighting. As will be seen, many of the iconic or intrinsic resemblances one may discern in movement research are based on the formal or qualitative aspects of the movement, while "what is done," or *"content,"* appears to be far more variable and ambiguous.

The relationship between the character or quality of a movement and what it is associated with may be very subtle and complex; and the movement referent may not be easily observable or have a "folk meaning" readily perceived and understood by "naive" observers. For example, I once witnessed Irmgard Bartenieff make a correct prediction of depression and suicidal behavior from observing the persistent movement rhythms of a woman she did not know and could not hear (but who on the surface appeared very lively and vivacious). There was a repeated pattern, seen throughout her gestures and actions, of lightning quick starts followed by channeled, direct bound movements that was interpreted as a kind of squelching of her energy and impulses. This is an example of interpreting qualitative or process features of the movement irrespective of content; it is also an interpretation that only someone highly trained in movement observation would be able to make.

In the literature, the major proponent of the arbitrary case is Birdwhistell. Birdwhistell maintains that the relationship between a movement and its meaning can only be determined by an analysis of when the movement occurs, in what contexts, and with what other behaviors in the communication stream. He takes the rigorous position that one must assume ignorance of the significance of movements and decipher the culture's meaning for any movement bit in relation to other same-size bits, then in relation to increasingly larger bits, just as structural linguists analyze language. It appears that Birdwhistell would argue that there is rarely a relationship between the nature of the movement and its deciphered meaning, that, as with abstract mathematical symbols devised to represent operations, there is usually no resemblance between the character of the behavior and its meaning. Put most simply and extremely this would be like saying kinesics is rarely "onomatopoetic," (Birdwhistell, 1970, p. 125).

Ekman and Friesen appear to regard many patterns as iconic. For example, they consider "bringing the two hands together to propose greater intimacy" a "spatial iconic code," and movements that draw pictures of events or objects are also iconic (Ekman and Friesen, 1969, p. 62). They consider rhythmic relationships between a movement and the phrase it is accenting iconic; and they maintain that many conventional gestures are either arbitrarily or iconically coded. But with many examples, such as facial expressions, they do not specify, calling them either iconically or intrinsically coded. One cannot consider Ekman and Friesen to be strict proponents of iconic relationships because they define iconic somewhat differently than is done here, and because frequently they say a pattern could be either iconic or intrinsic. Nevertheless they are researchers who actively entertain the possibility that the relationship between an action and its meaning may often be one of resemblance, extrinsically derived.

In many cases the intrinsic aspect of a movement may be only a part or a quality of it; to propose that there are intrinsic relationships to be found in a vast range of movement observations doesn't negate the possibility of concomitant arbitrary associations or situational factors that influence the significance of the movement pattern. One could use Frijda's research to illustrate this point. Frijda examined patterns of observer judgments of facial expressions and found that there were "invariable," or intrinsic, meanings attributed, and that situational cues had effects that gave the interpretations greater specificity and accuracy (Frijda, 1961). This thesis maintains that Frijda's conclusions are true for all types of movement and nonverbal behavior, and not just for facial expression— that there are intrinsic elements in various nonverbal patterns as well as situational factors and extrinsically derived features, and that the difficulty becomes one of analyzing phenomena that language doesn't adequately describe.

For example, Birdwhistell argues that a body "can be bowed in grief, in humility, in laughter, or in readiness for aggression" (Birdwhistell, 1970, p. 34), and presumably considers this as evidence for the arbitrariness of movement forms. However, each case shares an underlying common theme of "containing oneself," whether it is associated with making oneself smaller in humility, holding oneself together in grief, preventing oneself from "busting a gut" laughing, or collecting oneself in preparation for attack. Further, the specific examples may also vary in how one bows, each qualitative difference perhaps being visibly related to a different meaning. A humble bow may be done arms parallel to the side, head leading, the movement smooth and controlled. Bowing in grief or in laughter may be done with arms tensely clutching one's sides, the whole body contracting, but with the rhythm of breathing and "shaking" different in each case. Bowing in readiness to fight may involve a tight holding, but not the trembling or shaking of grief or laughter, and must of necessity involve outward focus. Knowledge of the situation would undoubtedly help in determining what exactly the particular bowing is associated with. However, the basic underlying pattern and the qualitative details of the movement itself may be a source of information as to its significance, as is an understanding of the context in which the movement occurs.

ARBITRARY VS. ICONIC OR INTRINSIC

Literature Evidence

A relationship is termed "arbitrary" when there is no apparent visual resemblance between a movement and its significance. The research presents numerous examples that do not seem arbitrary. For example, Charny discusses how certain congruent postural relationships observed in psychotherapy reflect "rapport" and greater relatedness and correspond with verbal behavior that is more "interpersonally oriented, positive, and specific" (Charny, 1966, p. 314). He delineates two types of "congruent" postures—"mirroring" (one person's position is the mirror image of the other) and "matching" (identical positions, with right matching right and left matching left)—and he distinguishes between upper and lower body congruence. Charny found that upper body mirror congruent relationships increased over time and correlated with speech content suggesting greater rapport and relatedness. "Noncongruent" posture periods were characterized by a "greater frequency of self-centered, negational, nonspecific lexical references" (Charny, 1966, p. 314). The connection here is apparent: congruence of position with rapport. If the relationship were arbitrary it might be "incongruent" positions with rapport.

Loeb (1968) describes how careful analysis of a film of a woman in psychotherapy shows that a "fist-like" gesture occurred only with verbal themes denoting anger, frustration, or fear of hurting her son. Again, one could ask why not hands folded, fingers crossed, or hand waving gently. The relationship doesn't seem arbitrary.

Exline and Winters (1965) found that subjects decreased eye contact with an experimenter who responded to their conversation negatively. Mehrabian (1969, p. 368) found a greater tendency for subjects to use an "arms-akimbo position" with low-status addressees. Again, one could ask why not decrease eye contact when one is neutrally reinforced, or why not stand erect and contained with "low-status addressees." The directions of these diverse findings would seem to oppose the idea that only arbitrary relationships exist, without visible resemblances between nonverbal behavior and that with which it is found to be associated.

Turning to the literature analyzed in Table 4 and considering the entries from specific movement categories, one may again see relationships that do not appear arbitrary. For example, one might take all the entries under the item "in-out" in the "spatial aspects" category. It is important to consider different nuances in the definition of "in-out" when examining how it is variously interpreted. Allport and Vernon are listed here because they derive a centrifugal factor from subjects' scores on various tests that they interpret "as a general 'outward-tendency,' freedom and 'extroversion' of expressive movement" (Allport and Vernon, 1933, p. 112). While they do not systematically correlate this quality with personality factors they note that it is higher among the younger subjects. When describing four cases they note that the individual with a very low centrifugal range has spacious and vivid movements that are not directed outward from the body and remark that "this man, though exceedingly expansive, is not of the administrative type or in the least egotistic" (Allport and Vernon, 1933, p. 139). A subject high in centrifugal features appeared to overstep "in the motor sphere, exactly as he does in the intellectual and social spheres" (Allport and Vernon, 1933, p. 143).

One can see a trend in this literature toward paralleling expansion with exploration, "reaching out to," etc., while contraction is associated in some way with "retraction from," self-protection, and making oneself smaller. Again, the nuance of the definition itself seems to "fit" the nuance of the interpretation made. In the case above "over-outwardness" becomes intrusiveness. Kestenberg attends to continual fluctuations in "growing and shrinking" as the individual's commerce with the world and regards it organismically:

> We change our shape by alternately growing and shrinking as we inhale and exhale. We grow as we take in and shrink when we ex-

pel waste. We grow toward pleasant stimuli and shrink away from noxious ones. (Kestenberg et al., 1972, p. 747)

Reich and Lowen appear to have a similar approach to interpreting general expansion and contraction patterns (Lowen, 1958, p. 43; Reich, 1949, p 358). While it is put in Reich's special terminology, the following quote alludes to a similar correlation:

> *Basically, emotion is an expressive plasmatic motion.* Pleasurable stimuli cause an "emotion" of the protoplasm from the center toward the periphery. Conversely, unpleasurable stimuli cause an "emotion"—or rather, "remotion"—from the periphery to the center of the organism. (Reich, 1949, p. 358)

There is a tendency in these writers to regard "in-out" in a very general way as related to basic life functioning and to discuss the importance of growing-shrinking or expansion-contraction patterns in terms of general theories of affect and emotion. However, one also finds specific examples that tie this line of interpretation to actual situations. For example, North interprets a child's "frequent inward flowing of movement" with emotional insecurity and inhibition (North, 1971, p. 126). To cite an interpersonal example, Scheflen describes the progression to "open" positions in terms of "accessibility for relationships" (Scheflen, 1965, p. 50).

It would require another volume to analyze the 17 works in terms of the resemblances between the movements observed and their possible "meanings" or "significances." For purposes of this discussion I will examine one more parameter this way. In Table 4 one finds nine authors listed under the qualitative term "forceful" (vigorous, strong). Again, they are very different studies and the movement examples that contain references to "forceful" are quite diverse. Yet one can "hear" something shared in their interpretations of "forceful". (It is important to note here that "forceful" refers to intensity or impact not to "large mass," great tension, or heaviness, as will be seen in the examples.)

Allport and Vernon use measures of pressure or force in their series of experimental tests for consistency of movement style. The individual who scored very high in "forcefulness" and was first on the "emphatic" group factor (which was drawn largely from pressure and force measures) was a man described as aggressive and self-confident with a capacity for delay and a need to be certain before committing himself (Allport and Vernon, 1933, p. 136).

Lowen discusses how "oral characters" tire rapidly when "hitting a couch"; they feel they lack energy (Lowen, 1958, p. 173). He appears to regard this difficulty with making strong actions as one of a number of physical correlates of the "oral character's" inability to be aggressive (p. 178). Here "aggressive" is used not in the destructive sense but in the sense of assertion, engaging the environment, actively getting one's needs met (p. 178).

Reich refers to force when discussing the inability of the "armored individual" to express primitive biological emotions such as "hitting the couch in anger" (Reich, 1949, p. 366). Darwin (1872) also describes force in relation to expression of strong emotions such as rage (p. 239) or "excessive grief" (p. 176). A patient described by Mahl as often gesturing formed, such as pressing and squeezing the arm of the chair, as reflecting a "great deal of hostility" outward and against herself (p. 308).

Mahl interpreted the variety of "hostile" acts that a woman patient performed, such as pressing and squeezing the arm of the chair, as reflecting a "great deal of hostility" outward and against herself (p. 308).

Birdwhistell describes an interaction between a mother and her child in which the increasing insistence of the child was characterized by "jerking" the mother's sleeve, clenching his fists and pulling them "with stress against his chest," grabbing the mother's arm tightly, etc. This was met by slaps and squeezes from the mother (Birdwhistell, 1970, pp. 284-285).

North presents a direct motion factor analysis of force considered as a predominant quality of one's movement. She distinguishes three degrees: "lessened strength," which she correlates with "weakening of will power"; "strong," correlated with "resolute, strong-willed"; and "very cramped strength," correlated with "exaggerated stubbornness" and "perhaps brutal" (North, 1971, p. 237).

Force is also used as a parameter to simply distinguish between groups, as when Efron observed that the gestures of his Italian subjects were more forceful or emphatic than those of Jews (Efron, 1941, p. 101), or when Lomax et al. included force in scales for degree of variation in "effort" or "disposition of energy in behavior" (Lomax, Bartenieff, and Paulay, 1968, pp. 271-272).

One sees in these nine examples a rather uniform perception of the significance of force in movement. Even Lomax et al., who do not interpret specific movement patterns in the way the others do, note that a "predominance of strength and/or speed" to the exclusion of other types of intensity is commonly found in the movements of "hunters, fishers, and incipient producers" (Lomax et al., p. 272). Whether or not force is given a negative connotation such as brutal or hostile depends on the degree to which it is overstressed, on the way it is used, and perhaps on the attitudes of the researcher. Nevertheless, one finds a common theme, something like impact-assertion-"substantiality."

No claim is made here that ultimately it will be possible to analyze movements according to a limited number of rules or formulae. In spite of some consistent lines of interpretation for specific parameters, movement is far too complex to be "reduced" to fixed meanings. The myriad combinations and sequences of movement variables as they continually occur militates against this; different combinations yield different nuances of meaning in spite of certain general "threads." Like the infinite variety of colors that emerge from mixtures of the primary colors, movement continually reveals an unlimited variety of patterns and combinations of its finite parameters. Thus "force" may be a primary motion element and may have a certain general range of meaning but may still occur within movement gestalts of quite different significances.

Different Types of Correlations

The literature examples presented above represent fairly specific one-to-one correlations between movements and what they are associated with. However, much of the literature previously reviewed does not present interpretations of specific actions or single variables. Under careful examination, the studies can be roughly divided into five types,[1] those which:

(1) analyze "articulation" and organization or patterning of the movement per se;
(2) primarily analyze the complexity of the movement;
(3) treat differences in movement patterns primarily for purposes of identifying or distinguishing between groups;
(4) examine developmental stages or progressions in movement;
(5) make specific interpretations either of the "instrumental" type or the pure motion factor type.

For example, under the "Body Part" category of the lexicon one finds studies that attend to discrete articulations of body parts, and their organization and patterning as they relate to speech structure and articulation (Birdwhistell, Kendon, Scheflen, and Condon)—i.e., it isn't so important *which* body part does the movement or what a body part "signifies" so much as how the medley of various body parts move and change in ways which somehow correspond to aspects of speech structure and patterning. This seems in some way to be the movement analogue of speech phonol-

[1] Of course a given study may involve some combination of these various types.

ogy and syntax, with "meaning," or "semantics," de-emphasized. If there is a general significance to what Condon and Birdwhistell discover through their "microanalyses," to what Kendon indicates with his speech motion analysis, and to what Scheflen delineates with his larger kinesic units, it appears to be that movement is intricately patterned at many levels and that, at least with respect to movement that occurs during speech, it may in some ways correlate with speech syntax, reflecting the beginning and ending of communication units and corresponding to various levels of speech structure.

Still looking at entries under "Body Part," one can find a study (Lomax, Bartenieff, and Paulay) that observes body parts largely in terms of what and how many parts are predominantly moved, and considers this to be a measure of complexity. That is, the more parts that are actively articulated, the more complex is the movement. This, along with other movement indices of complexity, is correlated with the complexity of the culture's subsistence type. Again "which" parts is not primary and significance is not attributed to the body parts themselves; what is focused on is how many as an indication of how complex.

A third possibility, and this may be found in a work such as Efron's comparison of Italian and Jewish movement styles, considers which body parts are moved as a reflection of population differences, something akin to "identifiers." In this case, noticing which body parts are moved becomes one way of discriminating between individuals or groups and the particular body parts are primarily regarded as "identifiers," but interpretation is not made of the parts or their uses themselves.

A fourth possibility is looking at body part movement patterns as reflections of developmental progression. For example, Gesell notes that in a study of the development of the sitting posture, "neuro-motor organization of the trunk proceeds in a head-to-foot direction" (Gesell, 1940, p. 67). Here "what body parts" is examined in terms of developmental stages or progressions. This would include observations of a progression from total body reaction patterns to increasingly more discrete localized reactions or to proximal-to-distal developments.

When it comes to more specific "meaning," there are, roughly speaking, two different types: "instrumental" and "motion factor" interpretations. An instrumental interpretation is an analysis that infers or experimentally determines a direct connection between a movement and some specific activity of which it is a "vestige" or derivation. Many of Darwin's interpretations are of this type, such as when he traces making a fist and clenching the jaw to a total action pattern of preparation for fighting. Reich and Lowen also make "instrumental" interpretations when they term certain chronic postures or facial expressions "frozen" preparatory or defensive attitudes, vestiges of action patterns that were once adaptive to some strong affect or situation periling the integrity of the individual. To return to the body part parameter, in relation to instrumental interpretations, the question of which body part is crucial to the association because the particular biological or emotional potential(s) of the part determine the interpretation. The intricate psychoanalytic interpretations of Reich and Lowen depend in large part on a consideration of the function of the body part—for example, chronic immobility of the pelvic area may be regarded as symptomatic of sexual repression (Reich, 1949, p. 389), or expressions of the throat and mouth area may be associated with the natural functions of this area: sucking, biting, vomiting, etc. Here psychological interpretations of specific constrictions are in part determined by extrapolating from the functions of that part or area. Darwin also does this when he characterizes certain facial expressions according to the activities from which they seem to be derived. For example, frowning (contracting the brows) in deep thought is traced to protecting the eyes as one scans the horizon (Darwin, 1872, pp. 224-226). Deutsch and Mahl also appear to derive their clinical analyses partly from a consideration of the function of the particular body part that is performing the act. For example, Deutsch repeatedly interprets leg movements as a way of defending against genital impulses (as opposed to arm movements) (Deutsch, 1947).

The second type of specific interpretation is a difficult and elusive one to discuss—namely, the significance of "pure motion factors or features" in and of themselves, apart from their role in specific, functional actions, and apart from considerations of complexity, articulation, identification-per-se, or developmental progressions. For example, a sequence of movements may be done in a particular "rhythm" such as quick to slow to sinuous and quick again. Ekman and Friesen cite the rhythmic relationship that "traces the flow of an idea or accents a particular phrase" and state that in their usage of the term "rhythmic" these iconic patterns carry "no message content apart from information about tempo." (Ekman and Friesen, 1969, p. 62). However, one could regard the elements of rhythm such as force, tempo, etc., as well as spatial directions, planes, and types of body part organization, as motion factors with potential meanings, though these meanings can be only roughly alluded to or approximated with words. There are some studies that consider these factors in and of themselves irrespective of the context or the action in which they are embedded, as in the interpretations of the "force" and "in-out" variables previously discussed.

In terms of body parts an example of this kind of interpretation would be to regard a predominance of postural vs. gestural movements as a reflection of the degree of interpersonal or emotional involvement (Davis, 1964). That is, movement-through-entire body vs. movement-limited-to-a-part is correlated with interpersonal involvement. An obvious example would be a handshake in which one moved only the head and forearm vs. a handshake that "reverberated" through the entire body.

Formal resemblances between the movement observations and what they are associated with in each of these ways of interpreting may be demonstrated as below:

Number of parts as a measure of complexity	Aspects of cultural complexity
Types of articulation and patterning of body parts	Articulation and delineation of communication units
Which parts move per se	Identification or discrimination of individuals or groups per se
Stages of predominance of a particular part	Developmental stages
Instrumental potential or biological function of a part or area	Expression of emotions, relationship to problems of "orality," "genitality," etc.
Body part organization or motion factor per se	Psychological phenomena such as degree of involvement

While some of these relationships are so diffuse or general as to be weak illustrations of iconic or intrinsic resemblances, one could at least argue that the studies that elucidate such correlations do not support the arbitrary position.

To conclude this section on the question of whether only arbitrary relationships exist between a movement and its significance(s), I will return to Birdwhistell who has been suggested as essentially a proponent of this position. Birdwhistell considers that his research in kinesics counters earlier research that assumes resemblances between a movement and its meaning(s). However, a close examination of his observations reveals a number of formal resemblances between the movement patterns and what they are associated with. His examples may be divided into those that:

(1) deal with speech-motion relationships at a "micro" level of detail. Here, stress patterns in speech are paralleled with stress patterns in movement; (referred to previously as Birdwhistell₁)

(2) serve to identify or distinguish one group from another, as in distinctions between male and female tertiary sexual characteristics; (Birdwhistell₂)

(3) deal with interaction at a minute level of detail as in mother-infant interactions. (Birdwhistell₁)

Much of the time he does not discuss significance, pointing out instead the enormous variability and cultural specificity of motion patterns. As such, the examples listed above do not constitute an argument for arbitrary relationships: stress patterns are correlated with stress patterns in the speech-motion examples; differences in movement characteristics are merely delineated in the sex differences example; or Birdwhistell may indirectly suggest meaning. When he does imply or state possible significance(s) for the patterns he observes, his interpretations do not appear arbitrary. For example, he suggests distal movements frontward may correlate with future tense verbs, while distal movements backward accompany past tense verbs (Birdwhistell, 1970, p. 123). The conflicting or opposing movements of the mother while diapering her child are followed by flailing by the child and "confusions" in the interaction example. And to return to the example of the hitchhikers mentioned earlier. If one visualizes exactly what they are doing, one gets an image of two young men thumbing with their "legs akimbo," fingers of one hand hooked into their belts, the other hand thumbing in what appears to be a twisting motion (i.e., not just a side sweep with the thumb up). The driver "flares his nostrils," reveals his upper teeth, and rapidly thrusts his head back, which apparently leads to an "Italian salute" from one of the passed-by soldiers (p. 176). Birdwhistell goes on to discuss the "insultingly rejective activity" of the driver (p. 178) and the "male defiant" stance of the soldiers, who apparently occupy a "different American male subculture role" than do college students who thumb a ride with an "ingratiating stance and head cock plus smile" (p. 179). These correlations appear to be anything but arbitrary.

In the previous section evidence was presented to refute the contention that the relationships between a movement and its meaning(s) are primarily arbitrary. This does not necessarily mean that arbitrary relationships are never found. In fact, it would seem that very fixed, specific gestures such as sign conventions, or what Ekman and Friesen call "emblems" (Ekman and Friesen, 1969, p. 63) and define as "those nonverbal acts which have a direct verbal translation, or dictionary definition, usually consisting of a word or two, or perhaps a phrase" (p. 63), are often likely to be arbitrary. Perhaps of all the literature, the work by LaBarre listing cultural gestures having specific meanings most clearly illustrates arbitrary associations (LaBarre, 1964). In this work LaBarre cites numerous gestures and their meanings, and in many cases one cannot discern any resemblances. For example, he says that "the Copper Eskimo welcomes strangers with a buffet on the head or shoulders with the fist" (p. 199); protruding tongues signify wisdom in Mayan statues of the gods (p. 200); and tapping the right forefinger to the right nostril meant amused incredulity in the 18th century (p. 203). In many of his examples one may see vestiges of resemblances or visible associations but apart from these one may consider the gesture conventions as so specific and limited that they are subject to great variation and "mutation" and may be derived from associations and events long since lost or undetectable. Just as verbal content is highly variable and it is difficult, if not impossible, in most cases to discern relationships between the word sound and its significance, gesture conventions often have very specific meanings that may become arbitrary over time. For example, they may begin with iconic or intrinsic resemblances but acquire very specific meanings that become "frozen" and susceptible to associations with other meanings with which they do not have a resemblance. Or, the initial association may be a special local one that cannot be recognized elsewhere, such as imitating a figure or an object. Again, iconic and intrinsic relationships are more apparent when one attends to the formal qualitative or process aspects of the movement and not to its specific "content."

ICONIC VS. INTRINSIC

Acknowledging these few examples of arbitrary relationships and considering the wealth of data supporting resemblances, the question next becomes: Are the resemblances more likely to be iconic (and extrinsic) or intrinsic? Here the argument must mainly be a theoretical one. The iconic relationship is one where there are visible resemblances between the movement and its significance, but these are merely resemblances somehow derived extrinsically, as in the case of a movement gesture having a certain form because it was found to be more efficient or clearer as a signal if its form resembled its significance. For example, football referees' signs would appear to be largely iconic. If iconic is taken to mean externally derived by some process of signal derivation, as with the football signs, then there are a number of arguments against iconic resemblances relative to most of the research analyzed in Chapter IV.

Parsimony

Consider the possibility of a relationship between contracting the stomach muscles and holding one's breath and the feelings of anxiety and fear. To posit that this relationship is iconic would not appear parsimonious. That is, to say that the muscle contractions became associated with anxiety according to some external process of association or learning of a cultural convention would not seem the most parsimonious explanation. To take another example, to assume that facial expressions are iconic and that one somehow learns to associate pleasure with smiling or anger with frowning would seem to pass over the developmental and functional significance of such patterns. In the first case, contracting the stomach muscles and holding one's breath can readily be seen to be functional, a way of coping with a painful experience. In the second example, it would seem more parsimonious to argue that smiling is intrinsically related to pleasure in the sense that it is a free, widening, expanding movement, whereas frowning in distress or anger is a tight, contracting motion. The intrinsic interpretation makes possible developmental and evolutionary explanations and aids in the determination of the movement's adaptive function. This is not to say that the expression may not take on other associations and evolve as a communicative "signal" for that with which it originally was associated. The model on TV may smile a great deal to signify pleasure and friendliness without "meaning" it; the point is that one sees in development and evolution, as well as in numerous adaptive actions of adults, many relationships between a given movement and its significance that appear to be intrinsic. To consider most of the resemblances cited previously to be iconic and extrinsic would seem to require an even more elaborate and roundabout explanation of their existence.

Isomorphism

Another theoretical argument for intrinsic significance is the possibility of isomorphic relationships occurring at different levels. That is, it would make sense that certain patterns persist across levels, contributing a kind of coherency and organization to nonverbal behavior from the intra-organismic level to social and cultural levels. There is already some evidence for this. For example, synchrony or clear simultaneity in movement may be observed at the individual level, between the individual and his speech (Condon and Ogston, 1967); between one individual and another ("interactional synchrony," Condon and Ogston, 1967); at large group levels (as in all dancing, marching, walking, or cheering together synchronously); and even at a cultural level in the sense of everyone performing similar acts on a national holiday. The "meaning" of synchrony is not simple. But when one examines what different researchers associate it with at different levels there is a kind of isomorphism that suggests its general significance. Condon finds that dyssynchrony of body parts in relation to one another is found in schizophrenic patients (Condon and Ogston, 1966). Davis also finds a significant correlation between what she calls movement "fragmentation" and a diagnosis of schizophrenia in conjunction with a history of more than two hospitalizations (Davis, 1970). Condon states that movement synchrony between individuals is a common feature of interaction and he seems to regard it as an element of "getting together" and group integration (Condon, 1968). Meerloo talks about similar rhythmic movements occurring in large groups as a kind of "group contagion" (Meerloo, 1964).

Finally, one could consider a shared action of an entire culture, as during a holiday, to be in some way a reflection of a shared life style or common identity. While this last is a rather trite, simplistic example, it is cited here to complete the argument—i.e., there may be formal parallels from the "organismic" level to the cultural one. This "synchrony" of action may be considered on different levels but may still share a common thread—something akin to "getting it together," "integration," or "common identity"—as follows:

Cultural—i.e., same action on a holiday	Shared life style, common identity
Large group or crowd all moving together (as in "mass contagion," Meerloo, 1961)	Shared feeling
Small group level—e.g., movement synchrony among individuals (Condon, 1968)	Momentary relatedness or rapport

Individual level—e.g., body parts moving in synchrony with each other (Condon, 1968; Davis, 1970)	Ego integration

Similar parallels may be found with other movement parameters. For example, contraction-expansion occurs as a fundamental pattern within the organism. As discussed earlier (under interpretations of the in-out dimension) it may be regarded "organismically" to reflect general patterns, such as growing in pleasure or contracting in displeasure, or it may have very specific referents, such as high centrifugal motor patterns being associated with the personality trait "over-intrusive" (Allport and Vernon, 1933, p. 142). At the group level one may posit a parallel between the in-out dimension and movements toward and away. Then general patterns toward and away may reflect closeness or approach vs. moving away from others and towards self, as in Scheflen's associating a position which is closer and more open with "accessibility for relationships" (Scheflen, 1965, p. 50).

A number of parameters may have "cross-level" forms. "Synchrony" and "in-out" are two possibilities. "Verticality" is another. That is, vertical movements or stress on verticality within the individual mover has been associated with intrapsychic conflicts over control and self-assertion (cf. Reich, 1949, p. 181). The group-level concomitant might be "above or below another," which may be seen so often as a relevant parameter in status relationships (cf. bowing, fighting to put one's opponent "down," etc.). Parallels may be seen between body part relationships and group relationships. Irmgard Bartenieff[2] has pointed out that in an Indian group she observed on film, the pattern of moving two parts in relation to each other, as opposed to one body part still and the other part moving about it, is mirrored in group interaction. For example, the Indian man puts on his headpiece by turning the head in relationship to his circling arms (not holding the head still and moving the arms around). At the water well two Indian women can be seen moving together the same way, the first adjusting herself to the movement of the other placing the urn on her head (rather than holding still as the other moves). These parallels will be discussed further in the final chapter. At this point they are cited to support the argument that it would appear more parsimonious and consonant

---

[2] Irmgard Bartenieff, personal communication, 1972.

with biological systems to theorize that there are intrinsic relationships, as suggested by the isomorphism of resemblances across levels.

Central Organizing Principles

The intrinsic relationship is more consonant with the notion that movement patterns are reflections or inherent parts of central organizing processes, rather than series of additive bits accrued through some process of association or conditioning. For example, the association between forward movements (rather than backward or whatever) and future tense verbs might be understood as having evolved because of language conventions or some visual "signal" potential of the movement. However, a much more parsimonious explanation is that there is a profound, intrinsic relationship here having to do with central organizing processes in the system that controls our effort to communicate and comprehend "future." This assumes that the concept "future" is deeply embedded in some central construct that finds its expression in diverse modalities: linguistically in future tense verbs, motorically in forward movement accompanying the use of future tense verbs, visually perhaps in vista perception (Fk) on the Rorschach, and so on. A further implication is that this is true for all sorts of movement patterns, from the relationships between movement and speech syntax to the relationships between muscle tension patterns and anxiety. To posit otherwise would seem to require very cumbersome, far-fetched explanations for the numerous resemblances that can be discerned between movements and their significance(s).

Some movements such as pointing, "drawing a picture" in space, or imitating some characteristic of an object or person in order to designate them are perhaps closest to the case in which the movement is merely a "sign" for something and so would best be regarded as iconic. But such movements are a relatively small part of the continual motion one sees and most of the literature analyzed in the previous chapters does not deal with these to any great extent.

CONCLUDING REMARKS

Historically one can see a marked shift in movement research that was initiated by Birdwhistell in the early 1950's. He was iconoclastic and one of the forms his iconoclasm took as a rejection of earlier studies of movement in relation to personality or emotional expression. Studies of "isolated examples of vocalic variation or gesture and posture as expressional behavior" (and this seems to include most of the major movement research before 1950) are not of "direct concern" to Birdwhistell; their "patent ethnocentrism, atomism, or biologism has precluded rather than encouraged cross-cultural study." (Birdwhistell, 1970, p. 38) It appears that Birdwhistell regards most of the research regarding movement-qua-expression as not only irrelevant to the "linguistic-kinesic approach to micro-cultural analysis" (p. 39) but as misleading and detrimental to it.

As has been said, Birdwhistell's innovations have extended movement research into profoundly important areas largely ignored before him, and he has certainly been a prime mover in the current renaissance in body movement research. However, at this point one could argue that Birdwhistell at his purest and most iconoclastic has thrown out the baby with the bathwater. It is time that the baby be reclaimed without denying the importance of the reasons why Birdwhistell heaved the bathwater.

There are major differences between kinesics as conceptualized by Birdwhistell and earlier writing on movement such as by Darwin, Reich, or Allport and Vernon. Some of the differences are in parameters used, levels of observation, and methodology. And of course they are interested in different subjects. But at times the conflicts between the "expressionists" and the "communicationists" appear to be empty. For example, of course there would be differences between research that focused on minute variations in movement relative to culture, social role, context, and what is being said and research that focused on consistencies that persist in an individual's movement across contexts. But there are some basic theoretical differences that appear to underlie Birdwhistell's rejection of these earlier writings and that bear examination. Among them is the assumption that there are perceptible resemblances between a movement and its significance, an assumption apparently held by the expressionists (and perhaps by some current researchers such as Ekman and Mehrabian) and rejected by Birdwhistell (and perhaps by Scheflen).

Much of the research discussed in this chapter is psychological and "expressionist," and so it might not be surprising that it provides many examples of iconic or intrinsic resemblances. The argument might well be that it is a different level, an "organismic" or intrapsychic one, whereas Birdwhistell is concerned with communication and cultural variation in movement. Then, if so, and if one accepts the value of both levels of research, one is faced with the possibility that movement patterns relative to intrapsychic processes, emotion, or personality are intrinsic, whereas movement at the level of face to face interaction and communication "programs" are arbitrary. As asserted previously the observations cited by the "communicationists" do not yet clearly support the existence of arbitrary relationships. It would seem that "expression" vs. "communication" is a false dichotomy. What is needed are more complex and sophisticated ways of understanding the relationships between individual and cultural differences, and between the "intrapsychic" level in movement and the interpersonal one. Some ideas for such an integration will be proposed in the next chapter.

Chapter VII

THEORETICAL CONSIDERATIONS AND IMPLICATIONS FOR FUTURE RESEARCH

There are perhaps several agendas in this dissertation. The first has been a fairly technical one, to show that problems of description and accurate terminology are greatly neglected in most research on body movement. Thus, if one examines the terminology used, common sense shows that (a) there is great diversity within the studies simply in terms of description and what in movement is attended to and (b) because different researchers select different movement variables or delimit the same ones in different ways, one cannot yet assume that their results contradict or refute each other. So the first part of this work was discursive and rather matter-of-fact, however technical it might have become.

The second agenda, one which evolved from the first, was to examine the trend in very diverse studies of consistent relationships between the character of movement patterns and what they were associated with. Thus, one finds a certain logic in the selection of motion parameters for given problems, and further, one finds that there are perceptible resemblances between movements observed and their intrapsychic, interpersonal, or cultural significance(s). Without denying the complexity and the problems in such an analysis, this led to an examination of what have been regarded here as the intrinsic relationships one finds between the movements made and the interpretations given, even in communication-oriented research and studies of cross-cultural movement patterns.

It has been proposed that such intrinsic relationships may exist on diverse levels from intrapsychic to cultural without serious distortion or contradiction. However, it is important to be clear about what level one is focusing on, and about what actual behaviors, and what movement parameters if such relationships are to be identified. Furthermore, language often does not do justice to the phenomena; one can only allude to the intrinsic character of resemblances with more or less success, but the limitations of language and the danger of making facile, over-simplified interpretations does not negate the possibility that such relationships exist. Finally, it was stated that the existence of such intrinsic relationships does not rule out the possibility that the significance of movement is partly determined by the situation or by some extrinsic factors.

One might argue that there have also been some covert agendas here, among them an attempt to demonstrate the enormous complexity of movement and its potential for behavioral research. Hence, the elaborate charts illustrating the information that movement can yield and the overview including everything from developmental processes to cultural comparisons. The author's bias in favor of a movement terminology for movement research (as opposed to everyday language, linguistic concepts, etc.) is quite evident. Yet there has been an attempt here to present a rationale for and a demonstration of its efficacy, because this topic has not been extensively discussed in the research literature.

Before concluding I would like to develop this thesis two steps further theoretically. These are at best tentative extrapolations from the literature and from my own research experience: first, a conceptual model for the integration of several different lines of research, and second, proposals for an area of research that should prove productive if the analysis developed in this thesis is valid.

THEORETICAL MODEL FOR INTEGRATING DIVERSE AREAS OF MOVEMENT RESEARCH

Figure 1 is an attempt to outline the major research topics discussed according to the movement parameters, along two dimensions. It is possible to survey the movement research reviewed in terms of level (as has been done in Table 5) and also in terms of time, from momentary events to chronic, repeated patterns. That is, Figure 1 takes as its core or point of departure the movement variables themselves (see the center strip). They are intentionally arranged horizontally in order, from those which I will call "body level" parameters on the left to group movement variables on the right. As can be seen, these are parallel in the horizontal di-

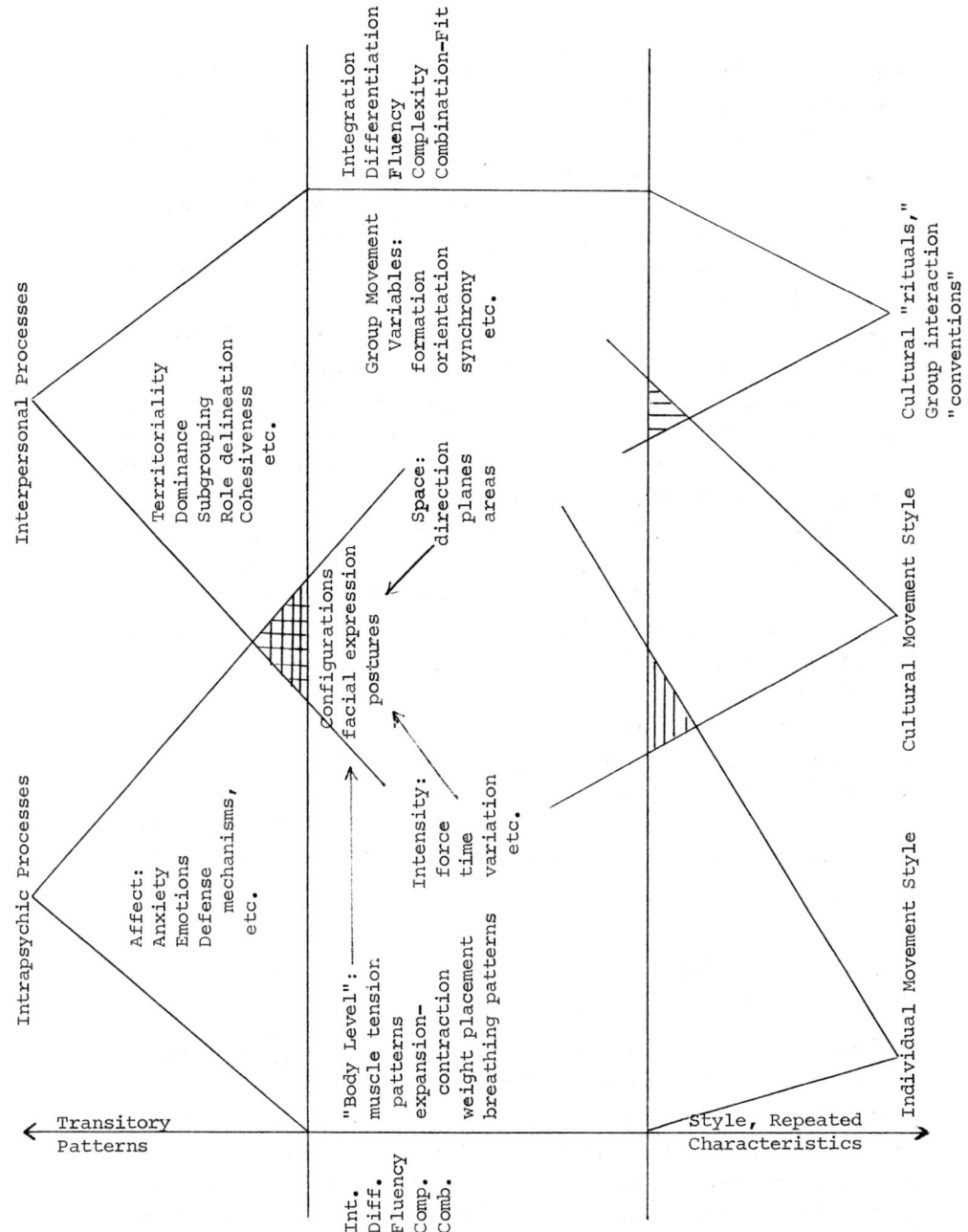

Figure 1. Theoretical Correlations Between Movement Parameters and Specific Behavioral Phenomena

mension by a progression from the intrapsychic to interpersonal level. Vertically there is a range from momentary change or event (in the upper areas of the diagram) to fixed, persistent patterns (represented in the lower areas of the diagram). The "body level" parameters are those aspects of movement that may be seen as the "substrates" of movement patterns in space. They include muscle tension patterns, expansion-contraction patterns such as in breathing, weight placement, and body coordination variables such as successive or simultaneous.[1]

Next to these, and directly developing out of them, are the "intensity" variables—movement qualities or variations in force, tempo, rhythm, etc. The next cluster, called here "configurations," is drawn in such a way as to indicate that it is somehow an amalgam of the other three clusters —"body level," "intensity," and "space" variables. Included in "configurations" are the more gestalt-like aspects of body movement such as body attitudes, positions, and facial expression—i.e., complex configurations of several movement parameters that can be perceived more or less as "gestalts" at any one moment (as opposed to the other variables, which are continuous fluctuations and "streams" of variation). These are what are most commonly illustrated with photographs because a photograph focuses on the configuration, not on the continuous movement. Below and to the right of "configurations" are the "space" variables such as variations in direction, planes, or areas of space around the mover. It will be seen here that "space" variables are placed at the nexus between the "group movement variables" and movement patterns that may be seen in the individual (or members of the same group) in many situations —talking, working, etc. The group variables include items such as group formation, orientation, group synchrony, etc.—variables that by definition refer to relationships between two or more people. As the diagram shows, most of the variables so far defined under this factor involve spatial relationships; hence, space variables per se are placed between the group variables and the rest of the variables.

The upper left of the diagram has a triangle drawn to indicate that when a study *primarily* deals with "body level" "intensity," and/or configurations such as facial expression, it often relates these to affect, arousal level, or intrapsychic dynamics such as defense mechanisms. In-

---

Note that this is a theoretical schema with approximations for the sake of discussion; it is not to be inferred that the "body level" patterns may not also vary relative to other levels, such as the interpersonal one. The diagram proposes approximations and predominant "realms."

cluded here, for example, would be muscle tension studies in relation to anxiety and studies in the recognition of emotion from facial expression. On the upper right part of the diagram, a triangle is drawn primarily to include configurations, space, and group movement variables in order to indicate that these are frequently related to group processes such as territorial behavior, dominance hierarchies, cohesiveness, and sub-grouping patterns. As the diagram indicates, studies that would fall under this area, such as Scheflen's analysis of the interaction in the family session, have virtually no variables in common with studies like Marion North's, which assesses individual movement styles mainly using "intensity" and "body level" parameters. In other words, from the point of view of what variables are selected, a study like Scheflen's is purely "interpersonal." However, as the diagram illustrates, there may be an interesting area of overlap, what will be called here the "interface" between the individual's movement patterns and the group nonverbal interaction. For example, if someone takes a particular position in a group, that position may be seen as a "coin" with two sides. From the point of view of the group, there is the total configuration, spacing, patterns of complementarity between positions, etc. of which that position is a part. However, the position on the other side of the coin may also be assessed relative to the individual mover, his repertoire of actions, and his means of coping with or adapting to intrapsychic processes and the "reverberations" within him of the interpersonal situation. The position is at the interface between the intrapsychic and the interpersonal. To take another example, the rigid, controlled body attitude that Reich describes in the aristocratic character is simultaneously a defense against (and in this way a reflection of) inner conflicts, as well as a mode of dealing with the outside world. The subject walks in and sits down in a measured, rigid way, his posture being at once an intra- and interpersonal statement (reflecting inner control and lending itself to noncongruent vertical relationships with the therapist's posture). This interface possibility would also be useful in explaining the expressions that Darwin assesses. To Darwin, facial expressions are vestiges of patterns that are at once reflections of emotion and adaptive actions; he simply does not concentrate on their interpersonal aspect. As the diagram is drawn, a number of variables may play a part in this "interface," having both interpersonal and intrapsychic aspects in a given situation.

The lower part of the diagram refers to what one "gets" when one considers the movement variables in terms of repeated characteristics—i.e., when the stylistic patterns of an individual or group are focused on. As has been discussed, the predominant patterns of an individual's movement may reflect individual and/or cultural differences. The degree to which they are cultural, "regional," or individual depends in part on the parameters used and on the degree of detail attended to. Thus, Efron's Italian subjects share characteristics X, Y, and Z, but within this group one might further distinguish individual A, who shows pattern X_{12}, Y_{23}, and Z_{32}, from Italian individual B, who shows movement patterns X_{23}, Y_{34}, and Z_{12}.

The lower left triangle suggests that studies focusing on individual differences concentrate on body level, intensity, configurations, and to a degree spatial predominances, while those studying differences in cultural styles utilize intensity, space, configurations, and group movement variables. There appear to be differences in stress and in degree of detail. As can be seen, there may be an area of overlap (indicated by the shading ≡≡≡), an area where the cultural and individual characteristics merge, as with Allport and Vernon's Italian subject. In cases like this one may hear references to something like "temperament," either cultural or individual. Notions of temperament may be used particularly, as the diagram suggests, when the variables used to distinguish cultural differences are intensity variables.

On the bottom far right is a triangle designated cultural "rituals" and group interaction "conventions"—"frozen" or fairly consistent patterns of group relationships. That is, one may study group formation as it varies from time to time or one may examine the more ritualized, conventionalized examples of nonverbal group relationships such as formation. Again, the diagram is drawn to suggest the possibility of an overlap between the cultural movement style per se and the culture's nonverbal rituals (see the area shaded |||||||||||||||||||||||||||). For example, a cultural movement style involving stress on single directions might overlap or interrelate with a predominance of single group line formations.

The terms written to the right and left of the "strip" of movement variables indicate that these patterns may be seen at all levels and throughout all variables. Of course, all of the movement variables may occur together all of the time and the diagram should not be taken as an illustration of what predominates at any one time or of what is more "advanced." In addition, properties of greater or lesser integration, differentiation, fluency, complexity, and, for want of a better term, what I will call "combination-fit" (i.e., the way the variables interrelate, complement, contrast, etc.) occur at different levels and across different variables. Thus, for example, one could examine degrees of fluency in the muscle tension patterns (cf. pauses, holds, abrupt changes vs. fluent transition), in the patterns of intensity, or in the spatial variations, and perhaps also in the group movement variables. This supports the assumption of an "isomorphism" across levels and parameters that can be seen in certain formal (non-content) patterns such as synchrony and degree of complexity.

Finally it may be noted that the diagram suggests relationships between affective processes and individual movement style and between interpersonal processes and cultural ritual. In a sense one could fold the upper half of the diagram over the lower half and see that the lower represents constant or recurring characteristics of the upper. Thus, for example, what for Darwin is a momentary postural adjustment in reaction to a fearful or threatening situation (e.g., holding breath, preparing to attack) becomes, when considered as a "chronic," persistent posture, one of Reich's muscular armors (e.g., a frozen defensive posture, shoulders held back, chest expanded, back rigid).

A POSSIBLE FUTURE DIRECTION FOR MOVEMENT RESEARCH

In the literature review of Chapter II it was pointed out that historically the early movement research concentrated on affective and personality factors in relation to movement and, as was subsequently shown, tended to focus on muscle tension patterns, chronic postures, patterns of intensity, and facial expression. Only in the last 20 years, thanks to Birdwhistell's innovations, has the focus shifted to group processes and consequently to group movement variables. I have tried to show that in a number of ways the communication orientation does not actually refute or replace the earlier studies, but supplements and complements them, at least at the level of description and with respect to the movement variables utilized. I would now like to go beyond past research to propose a direction suggested by this research and the analysis done in this dissertation that may prove productive and innovative in the future.

If one looks at the variables of the glossary and at the parameters as they are distributed in Figure 1, it is clear that the group movement variables are few in number compared to those that may be used to describe the movement of an individual (or movement characteristics shared by a group). In other words, the glossary of terms referring to movement relationships between people is as yet undeveloped. We have only the beginnings in terms such as "group synchrony," "mirror positions," "types of group formations," "proximity," etc. Yet we already know that these are important sources of information about group processes. Presumably, extending this list will enrich nonverbal research of group interaction (and perhaps cross-cultural studies of ritual and group interaction conventions).

If one holds that there is an isomorphism from one level to another, and that there are intrinsic relationships between various movement patterns and what they may be related to, then one source of ideas for new productive group parameters is the first part of the glossary. It has been pointed out that some variables have "parallels" on both the individual and group levels. For example one can talk about synchrony between the body part of a single mover or synchrony between two movers.[2] Another example is the in-out dimension where contraction-expansion patterns may be studied in the individual's movement, yet one could also examine patterns of toward and away between group members—i.e., toward and away from self to toward and away from each other.

I suspect that there are many more such parallels and that one way to develop the glossary of group movement variables is to pursue this process of extrapolation. For example, the vertical dimension of space may be focused on vis a vis the patterns of the mover (e.g., stress on verticality throughout one's actions) or vis a vis the vertical relationship between movers (e.g., higher vs. lower). The variety of spatial paths—straight, curved, serpentine, diagonal, etc.—seen in an individual's movement may also be seen in group formations. The body part relationships such as successive connections from one part to another vs. simultaneous movements may be paralleled in group interactions by such patterns as successive postural shifts by the group members vs. simultaneous shifts. I have already given the example of the Indian movement pattern that was observed on two levels—in the interplay of two body parts moving together (vs. one part stationery, the other surrounding it) and the same fluid, group relationship in which two people adjust to each other's movements (rather than one staying stationery and the other moving in relation to her).[3] It is also possible that there are parallels at the group level

---

[2] When I speak here of individual movement patterns I am referring to the movement per se as perceived either in an individual or in a number of individuals as opposed to variables that are defined according to relationships between two or more people. In this sense "individual movement variables" may refer to those used to define individual or cultural styles of moving.

[3] Irmgard Bartenieff, personal communication, 1972.

of the rhythmic patterns that can be seen in an individual's movement, from rapid changes in positions, orientations, and postural shifts to slow changes over a period of time. Deutsch occasionally refers to a patient who went through a rapid series of shifts before settling into one position (Deutsch, 1947). It is conceivable that group interactions vary "rhythmically" in similar ways.

Suggesting that group movement parameters parallel variables used to describe the movements of an individual does not mean that I am conceiving of a kind of transposing of intrapsychic processes onto the interpersonal level. They are to be thought of as two distinct levels that are defined by different variables and related by "isomorphic" formal parallels such as have been proposed. Conceivably, research might develop in such a way that one could as well define new individual parameters from group ones.

The implications for research of this distinction between individual parameters and group parameters are interesting. In the paradigm suggested by Figure 1, it might be possible to deduce one's relation to dominance hierarchies from one's individual movement characteristics, just as it may be possible to interpret individual personality dynamics from the group movement patterns one is involved in. However, theoretically this would represent a "second order inference." For example, if one says that A is "afraid" of B because A backs away from B, this would be an extrapolation from a parameter that by definition refers to the relation between A and B. As Scheflen's writing suggests, it makes more sense to study group processes from group parameters (Scheflen, 1965). In this case that would involve determining the nature of the relationship from the backward movement. That is, in theory it would be more powerful to predict a given process from the concomitant level of variables. If one found by focusing on the nonverbal relationships between A and B that they were in fact in a fighting relationship with B dominant over A, then it could be inferred that A is afraid here of B. But the inference of A's intrapsychic state from his movement relationship to B is less powerful. It would perhaps be more direct to predict that individual A is fearful because he very quickly contracts and holds his breath (i.e., attend to parameters on the left side of Figure 1). Focusing on A himself, the reverse situation would hold. That is, seeing someone quickly tense up and retract in space, one could infer that he is in an inferior or fighting relationship to someone not seen, but this would be a "second order inference." I dwell on this because such distinctions are frequently blurred in the research, making for controversies and ambiguities that could be sorted out if it were made clear at what level and from what parameters the interpretation or prediction is made.

One interesting line for future research may be the study of the relationships between the two levels—i.e., the correlations and contradictions between the individual's movement styles and the group nonverbal interaction of which he is a part. The way it is conceived here, the levels could influence each other, patterns of one "taking hold" on the other. For example, one can see in a film of the behavior of a child who developed schizophrenic symptomatology[4] that in infancy she had movement patterns characterized by a high degree of tension, repetition, and rapidity, and that this "rhythm" persisted over time in different forms. Also, at around three she could be seen to continually move away from others in a kind of shrinking, retreating action. This pattern seems to have become "frozen" in her posture in subsequent years in such a way that she no longer actively retreated, but her body attitude was a fixed, concave one, her weight back and her head held down and in throughout all her activity. The rhythm mentioned earlier shows up, conversely, in the high degree of repetitive, incessant action and the enormous difficulty she has in becoming synchronous (and therefore somewhat more modulated) with the movements of others. Conceptually, it would appear possible that the influence could go either way, the individual movement patterns influencing group interactions, as in the "rhythm" example, or the group interaction patterns affecting one's movement "repertoire," as in the "withdrawal" pattern described. Conceivably also there are many parallels in form from level to level. For example, a group of chronic schizophrenic individuals having movement characteristics that are reduced both in complexity and in integration could probably not orient to each other in complex formations and integrated patterns at the group level. As the diagram suggests, two of the most interesting questions may be: How do individual styles of moving relate to cultural movement characteristics? and How do individual and cultural movement styles relate to group interaction patterns?

CONCLUDING REMARKS

In this dissertation a wide range of research has been examined in the framework of the movement dimension itself. It is in part a demonstra-

---

[4] Film entitled, "Natural History of Psychotic Illness," Maudsley Hospital, distributed by New York University Film Library.

tion of the value of using a movement terminology rather than concepts and terms from other disciplines and of deriving theories about movement that are consonant with the nature of movement. Further, it would appear premature to develop theories of nonverbal communication on the basis of one area or function. For example, to focus primarily on the regulatory functions of movement would lead one to computer program analogies. But this has two dangers. First, the analogies may not apply to other aspects of movement, and second, movement itself is continuous and fluent in ways that may differ radically from program "units," and the regulation mechanisms may be quite different in kind. Similarly, it would be too great a step to construct theories about the general patterning and organization of movement from a study of its organization in relation to a special situation such as speaking. Movement patterns may be language-like in that they are in some ways composed of elements in combinations and sequences, but they may not be organized like language because the dimensions are qualitatively different in important ways. All this to say that there are dangers in drawing analogies or using methods from other disciplines for movement research. They may blur the unique properties of the dimensions of movement and observe what the study of movement may uniquely contribute to behavioral research. Further, it might be argued that mechanical models derived from such disciplines as computer technology would seem less appropriate than biological or even artistic models. It is notable that when Scheflen presents his analysis of the complex interrelationships of behaviors over time he appeals to the analogy of a musical composition with four voices in counterpoint and harmony (Scheflen, 1965).

Another conclusion one could draw from this dissertation is that people "see" very different aspects of movement and that the process of observation and description itself has methodological and theoretical implications.[5] As has been suggested, focusing on certain parameters to the exclusion of others leads one to certain kinds of information. The glossary helps provide a perspective on the wide range of variables one might consider, but is itself, of course, incomplete. One has to be continually aware

---

[5] Certainly one's discipline and training appears to effect his observations. No doubt there are cultural and personality determinants as well. It is my impression, for example, that among the current researchers, the men tend to observe movement quite differently from the women. The men appear to focus on position, instrumental actions (i.e., what is done), units, and spatial direction, while the women in this area are more likely to describe process, rhythmic patterns, and stylistic features.

of how one's focus, definitions, and method of recording may influence one's research.

One could make an argument for a very open-ended approach to movement research in the current movement renaissance—i.e., a reluctance to impose constructs or models drawn from other disciplines onto the movement research, and an openness to what different individuals observe and experience in movement. Chapters II and IV to the contrary, we really do not know very much yet about movement. What we do seem to know is that:

(1) it is a dimension of many variables that continually covary;

(2) it is related to developmental processes, affect, intrapsychic and interpersonal dynamics, and cultural differences;[6]

(3) it may be patterned, with smaller "bits" or variables combining into larger units, but we don't know yet how this can be because movements appear to be more "process" than "fixed" entities;

(4) there do not appear to be profound contradictions between what has so far been observed at the intrapersonal, interpersonal, and cultural levels, although there may be profound differences in the theoretical explanations of these observations.

---

[6] It may also be related to cognitive processes such as cognitive style or concept formation, but this is one of the least explored possibilities to date.

BIBLIOGRAPHY

Allport, G. W. and Vernon, P. E. *Studies in Expressive Movement,* New York: The Macmillan Company, 1933.

Argyle, M. Non-verbal communication in human social interaction. In: *Non-verbal Communication,* R. Hinde (Ed.) London: Royal Society and Cambridge University Press, forthcoming.

———, M. and Dean, J. Eye-contact, distance and affiliation. *Sociometry,* 1965, *28,* 289-304.

Barlow, W. Anxiety and muscle tension. In: *Modern Trends in Psychosomatic Medicine,* D. O'Neill (Ed.) New York: Paul B. Hoeber, 1955.

Bartenieff, I. and Davis, M. Effort-shape analysis of movement: the unity of expression and function. Unpublished monograph. Albert Einstein College of Medicine, 1965.

———, and Davis, M. An analysis of the movement behavior within a group psychotherapy session. Unpublished paper presented at the Conference of the American Group Psychotherapy Association, Chicago, 1968.

———, Davis, M., and Paulay, F. *Four Adaptations of Effort Theory in Research and Teaching.* New York: Dance Notation Bureau, 1972.

———, and Paulay, F. Choreometrics profiles. In: *Folk Song Style and Culture,* A. Lomax (Ed.) Washington, D.C.: American Association for the Advancement of Science, Publication No. 88, 1968.

Benesh, R. and Benesh, J. *An Introduction to Benesh Dance Notation,* London: A. & C. Black, 1956.

Birdwhistell, R. L. *Introduction to Kinesics,* Louisville, Ky.: University of Louisville Press, 1952.

———. *Kinesics and Context,* Philadelphia: University of Pennsylvania Press, 1970.

Bleuler, E. *Dementia Praecox or the Group of Schizophrenias,* New York: International Universities Press, 1950.

Braatöy, T. Psychology vs. anatomy in the treatment of "arm neuroses" with physiotherapy. *Journal of Nervous and Mental Disease,* 1952, *115,* 215-245.

Breuer, J. and Freud, S. *Studies in Hysteria,* 1895, reprint ed. New York: Basic Books, 1957.

Bühler, C. The social behavior of children. In: *A Handbook of Child Psychology,* C. Murchison (Ed.) Worcester, Mass.: Clark University Press, 1933.

Bull, N. *The Attitude Theory of Emotion,* 1951, reprint ed. New York: Johnson Reprint Corporation, 1968.

Canna, D. J. and Loring, E. *Kineseography: The Loring System of Dance Notation,* N.p.: Academy Press, 1955.

Charny, E. J. Psychosomatic manifestations of rapport in psychotherapy. *Psychosomatic Medicine,* 1966, *28,* 305-315.

Christiansen, B. *Thus Speaks the Body: Attempts Toward a Personology from the Point of View of Respiration and Postures,* Oslo, Norway: Institute for Social Research, 1963.

Clynes, M. On being in order. *Zygon: Journal of Religion and Science,* 1970, *5,* 63-84.

Condon, W. S. Linguistic-kinesic research and dance therapy. *American Dance Therapy Association Proceedings,* 1968, 21-44.

———, and Ogston, W. D. Sound film analysis of normal and pathological behavior patterns. *Journal of Nervous and Mental Disease,* 1966, *143,* 338-347.

———, and Ogston, W. D. A segmentation of behavior. *Journal of Psychiatric Research,* 1967, *5,* 221-235.

Darwin, C. *The Expression of the Emotions in Man and Animals,* 1872; reprint ed. Chicago: The University of Chicago Press, 1965.

Davis, M. A study and experiment in expressive movement. Unpublished paper, New York University, 1964.

———. An effort-shape movement analysis of a family therapy session. Unpublished paper, Yeshiva University, 1966.

———. Implications of general systems theory for research in psychology. Unpublished paper, Yeshiva University, 1967.

———. Movement characteristics of hospitalized psychiatric patients. Proceedings of the Fifth Annual Conference of the American Dance Therapy Association, 1970, 25-45.

———. *Understanding Body Movement: An Annotated Bibliography,* New York: Arno Press, 1972.

Davis, R. C. Methods of measuring muscular tension. *Psychological Bulletin,* 1942, *39,* 329-346.

Dell, C. *A Primer for Movement Description: Using Effort-shape and Supplementary Concepts,* New York: Dance Notation Bureau, 1970.

Deutsch, F. Analysis of postural behavior. *Psychoanalytic Quarterly,* 1947, *16,* 195-213.

———. Thus speaks the body: an analysis of postural behavior. *Transactions of the New York Academy of Sciences,* 1949, *12,* 58-62.

———. Analytic posturology. *Psychoanalytic Quarterly,* 1952, *21,* 196-214.

———. Some principles of correlating verbal and non-verbal communication. In: *Methods of Research in Psychotherapy,* L. A. Gottschalk and A. H. Auerbach (Eds.) New York: Appleton-Century-Crofts, 1966.

Duffy, E. Level of muscular tension as an aspect of personality. *Journal of General Psychology,* 1946, *35,* 161-171.

Duncan, S., Jr. Towards a grammar for floor apportionment: a system approach to face-to-face interaction. *Proceedings of the 2nd Annual Environmental Design Research Association Conference,* 1970, 225-235.

Efron, D. *Gesture and Environment,* New York: King's Crown Press, 1941.

Eibl-Eibesfeldt, I. Transcultural patterns of ritualized contact behavior. In: *Behavior and Environment: The Use of Space By Animals and Men,* A. H. Esser (Ed.) New York: Plenum Publishing Corporation, 1971.

Ekman, P. and Friesen, W. V. Nonverbal behavior in psychotherapy research. In: *Research in Psychotherapy,* Vol. III, J. M. Shlien (Ed.) Washington, D.C.: American Psychological Association, 1968.

———, and Friesen, W. V. The repertoire of nonverbal behavior: categories, origins, usage and coding. *Semiotica,* 1969, *1,* 49-98.

———, and Friesen, W. V. Constants across cultures in the face and emotion. *Journal of Personality and Social Psychology,* 1971, *17,* 124-129.

———, Friesen, W. V., and Tomkins, S. S. Facial affect scoring technique: a first validity study. *Semiotica,* 1971, *3,* 37-58.

———, Sorenson, E. R. and Friesen, W. V. Pan-cultural elements in facial displays of emotion. *Science,* 1969, *164,* 86-88.

Eshkol, N. *The Hand Book: The Detailed Notation of Hand and Finger Movements and Forms,* Tel Aviv, Israel: Movement Notation Society, 1971.

———, and Wachmann, A. *Movement Notation,* London: Weidenfeld and Nicholson, 1958.

———, Melvin P., Michl, J., Von Foerster, H., and Wachmann, A. *Notation of Movement,* Urbana: Biological Computer Laboratory, University of Illinois, 1970.

Exline, R. V. Explorations in the process of person perception: visual interaction in relation to competition, sex, and need for affiliation. *Journal of Personality,* 1963, *31,* 1-20.

———, Gray, D., and Schuette, D. Visual behavior in a dyad as affected by interview content and sex of respondent. *Journal of Personality and Social Psychology,* 1965, *1,* 201-209.

———, Thibaut, J., Brannon, C., and Gumpert, P. Visual interaction in relation to machiavellianism and an unethical act. *American Psychologist,* 1961, *16,* 396.

———, and Winters, L. C. Affective relations and mutual glances in dyads. In: *Affect, Cognition, and Personality,* S. S. Tomkins and C. E. Izard (Eds.) New York: Springer Publishing Co., 1965.

Ferenczi, S. Psycho-analytic observations on tic. *International Journal of Psycho-Analysis,* 1921, *2,* 1-30.

Freud, S. Symptomatic and chance actions. In: *The Basic Writings of Sigmund Freud,* A. A. Brill (Ed.) New York: Random House (Modern Library), 1938.

Fries, M. and Lewi, B. Interrelated factors in development: a study of pregnancy, labor, delivery, lying-in period and childhood. *American Journal of Orthopsychiatry,* 1938, *8,* 726-752.

Frijda, N. H. The understanding of facial expression of emotion. *Acta Psychologica,* 1953, *9,* 294-362.

———. Facial expression and situational cues. *Journal of Abnormal and Social Psychology,* 1958, *57,* 149-154.

———. Facial expression and situational cues: a control. *Acta Psychologica,* 1961, *18,* 239-244.

Frois-Wittman, J. The judgement of facial expression, *Journal of Experimental Psychology,* 1930, *13,* 113-151.

Gesell, A. and Ames, L. A. Early evidences of individuality in the human infant. *Scientific Monthly,* 1937, *45,* 217-226.

——— et al. *The First Five Years of Life,* New York: Harper & Row, 1940.

——— and Halverson, H. M. The daily maturation of infant behavior: a cinema study of postures, movements, and laterality, *Journal of Genetic Psychology,* 1942, *61,* 3-32.

Golani, I. and Zeidel, S. *The Golden Jackal,* Tel Aviv, Israel: Movement Notation Society, 1969.

Goodenough, F. L. The expression of emotion in infancy. *Child Development,* 1931, *2,* 96-101.

Goodman, N. *Languages of Art: An Approach to a Theory of Symbols,* Indianapolis: The Bobbs-Merrill Company, 1968.

Hall, Edward T. *The Hidden Dimension,* New York: Doubleday and Co., 1966.

Halverson, H. M. An experimental study of prehension in infants by means of systematic cinema records. *Genetic Psychology Monographs,* 1931, *10,* 107-286.

Hewes, G. W. World distribution of certain postural habits. *American Anthropologist,* 1955, *57,* 231-244.

Hunt, V. Neuromuscular structuring of human energy. Unpublished paper presented at the Forty-fifth Conference Program of the Western Society for Physical Education of College Women, 1970.

Hutchinson, A. *Labanotation or Kinetography Laban: The System of Analyzing and Recording Movement,* New York: Theatre Arts Books, 1970.

———. Survey and comparison of dance notation through the ages. Parts I and II. Unpublished paper, London, 1972.

Jacobson, E. *Biology of Emotions: New Understanding Derived from Biological Multidisciplinary Investigation; First Electrophysiological Measurements,* Springfield, Ill.: Charles C. Thomas, 1967.

Jarden, E. and Fernberger, S. W. The effect of suggestion on the judgement of facial expression of emotion. *American Journal of Psychology,* 1926, *37,* 565-570.

Jenness, A. The recognition of facial expressions of emotion. *Psychological Bulletin,* 1932, *29,* 324-350.

Kanner, L. Judging emotions from facial expressions. *Psychological Monographs,* Whole No. 186, 1931, *41,* 1-91.

Kendon, A. Some relationships between body motion and speech: an analysis of an example. In: *Studies in Dyadic Communication,* A. W. Siegman and B. Pope (Eds.) Elmsford, N.Y.: Pergamon Press, 1972.

———, and Cook, M. The consistency of gaze patterns in social interaction. *British Journal of Psychology,* 1969, *60,* 481-494.

Kestenberg, J. S. The role of movement patterns in development: II, flow of tension and effort. *Psychoanalytic Quarterly,* 1965, *34,* 517-563.

———. The role of movement patterns in development: III, the control of shape. *Psychoanalytic Quarterly,* 1967, *37,* 356-409.

———, Marcus, H., Robbins, E., Berlowe, J. and Buelte, A. Development of the young child as expressed through bodily movement. I. *Journal of the American Psychoanalytic Association,* 1971, *19,* 746-764.

Krout, M. H. A preliminary note on some obscure symbolic muscular responses of diagnostic value in the study of normal subjects. *American Journal of Psychiatry,* 1931, *88,* 29-71.

——— Autistic gestures: an experimental study in symbolic movement. *Psychological Monographs,* Whole No. 208, 1935, *46,* 1-126.

———. An experimental attempt to produce unconscious manual symbolic movements. *Journal of General Psychology,* 1954(a), *51,* 93-120.

———. An experimental attempt to determine the significance of unconscious manual symbolic movements. *Journal of General Psychology,* 1954(b), *51,* 121-152.

Kurath, G. P. Panorama of dance ethnology. *Current Anthropology,* 1960, *1,* 233-254.

Laban, R. *Principles of Dance and Movement Notation,* London: Macdonald & Evans, 1956.

———. *The Mastery of Movement,* L. Ullmann (Ed.) London: Macdonald & Evans, 1960.

———, and Lawrence, F. C. *Effort,* London: Macdonald & Evans, 1947.

La Barre, W. The cultural basis of emotions and gestures. *Journal of Personality,* 1947, *16,* 49-68.

———. Paralinguistics, kinesics, and cultural anthropology. In: *Approaches to Semiotics,* T. A. Sebeok, A. S. Hayes, and M. C. Bateson (Eds.) The Hague: Mouton & Co., 1964.

Lamb, W. and Turner, D. *Management Behaviour,* New York: International University Press, 1969.

Landis, C. The interpretation of facial expression of emotion. *Journal of General Psychology,* 1929, *2,* 59-72.

Lange, C. G. and James, W. *The Emotions,* Vol. I, Baltimore: The Williams and Wilkins Co., 1922.

Levy, D. M. *Behavioral Analysis: Analysis of Clinical Observations of Behavior, As Applied to Mother-Newborn Relationships,* Springfield, Ill.: Charles C. Thomas, 1958.

Loeb, F. F. The microscopic film analysis of the function of a recurrent behavioral pattern in a psychotherapeutic session. *Journal of Nervous and Mental Disease,* 1968, *147,* 605-617.

Lomax, A., Bartenieff, I. and Paulay, F. Dance style and culture. In: *Folk Song Style and Culture,* A. Lomax (Ed.) Washington, D.C.: American Association for the Advancement of Science, Publication No. 88, 1968.

———, Bartenieff, I. and Paulay, F. The choreometric coding book. In: *Folk Song Style and Culture,* A. Lomax (Ed.) Washington, D.C.: American Association for the Advancement of Science, Publication No. 88, 1968.

Loraas, O. I. The relationship of induced muscular tension, tension level and manifest anxiety in learning. *Journal of Experimental Psychology,* 1960, *59,* 145-152.

Lowen, A. *Physical Dynamics of Character Structure,* 1958, reprint ed. New York: The Macmillan Company, 1971.

———. *The Betrayal of the Body,* New York: The Macmillan Company, 1967.

Luria, A. *The Nature of Human Conflicts: An Objective Study of Disorganization and Control of Human Behavior*, W. H. Gantt (ed.) New York: Liveright Publishing Corp., 1932.

Mahl, G. F. Gestures and body movements in interviews. In: *Research in Psychotherapy*, Vol. III, J. M. Shlien (Ed.) Washington, D.C.: American Psychological Association, 1968.

Malmo, R. B., Boag, T. J., and Smith, A. A. Physiological study of personal interaction. *Psychosomatic Medicine*, 1957, *19*, 105-119.

―――, Shagass, C., Belanger, D. J. and Smith, A. A. Motor control in psychiatric patients under experimental stress. *Journal of Abnormal and Social Psychology*, 1951, *46*, 539-547.

―――, Smith, A. A. and Kohlmeyer, W. A. Motor manifestation of conflict in interview: a case study. *Journal of Abnormal and Social Psychology*, 1956, *52*, 268-271.

McGraw, M. B. *The Neuromuscular Maturation of the Human Infant*, New York: Columbia University Press, 1943.

Meerloo, J. A. M. Rhythm in babies and adults: its implications for mental contagion. *AMA Archives of General Psychiatry*, 1961, *5*, 169-175.

―――. *Unobtrusive Communication: Essays in Psycholinguistics*. A Assen, The Netherlands: Van Gorcum, 1964.

Mehrabian, A. Inference of attitudes from the posture, orientation, and distance of a communicator. *Journal of Consulting and Clinical Psychology*, 1968, *32*, 296-308.

―――. Significance of posture and position in the communication of attitude and status relationships. *Psychological Bulletin*, 1969, *71*, 359-372.

Mittlemann, B. Motility in infants, children and adults: patterns and psychodynamics. *Psychoanalytic Study of the Child*, 1954, *9*, 142-177.

Morris, M. *The Notation of Movement*, London: Kegan Paul, Trench, Trubner & Co., 1928.

North, M. *Personality Assessment Through Movement*, London: Macdonald & Evans, 1971.

Perls, F., Hefferline, R. F. and Goodman, P. *Gestalt Therapy: Excitement and Growth in the Human Personality*, New York: Dell Publishing Co., 1951.

Plutchik, R. The role of muscular tension in maladjustment. *Journal of General Psychology*, 1954, *50*, 45-62.

Preston-Dunlap, V. A notation system for recording observable motion. *International Journal of Man-Machine Studies*, 1969, *1*, 361-386.

Reich, W. *Character-Analysis*, New York: Farrar, Straus & Giroux (The Noonday Press), 1949.

Ruckmick, C. A preliminary study of the emotions. *Psychological Monographs*, 1921, *30*, 30-35.

Scheflen, A. E. The significance of posture in communication systems. *Psychiatry,* 1964, *27,* 316-331.

———. *The Stream and Structure of Communicational Behavior: Context Analysis of a Psychotherapy Session,* Behavioral Studies Monograph No. 1, Philadelphia: Eastern Pennsylvania Psychiatric Institute, 1965.

Schlosberg, H. Three dimensions of emotion. *Psychological Review,* 1954, *61,* 81-88.

Singleton, W. T. The change of movement timing with age. *British Journal of Psychology,* 1954, *45,* 166-172.

Spitz, R. A. *No and Yes: On the Genesis of Human Communication,* New York: International Universities Press, 1957.

———, and Wolf, K. M. The smiling response: a contribution to the ontogenesis of social relations. *Genetic Psychology Monographs,* 1946, *34,* 57-125.

Swan, C. Individual differences in the facial expressive behavior of preschool children: a study by the time-sampling method. *Genetic Psychology Monographs,* 1938, *20,* 557-650.

Takala, M. Studies of psychomotor personality tests, I. *Annales Academie Scientiarum Fennicae Sarja-Ser. B Nide-Tom 81,* 1953, *2,* 1-130.

Tomkins, S. S. *Affect Imagery Consciousness.* Vol. I, *The Positive Affects,* New York: Springer Publishing Co., 1962.

Washburn, R. W. A study of the smiling and laughing of infants in the first year of life. *Genetic Psychology Monographs,* 1929, *6,* 397-537.

Wolff, C. *A Psychology of Gesture,* London: Methuen & Co., 1945.

APPENDIX I

*Descriptions of the Seventeen References
Used for Glossary Analysis*

DESCRIPTIONS OF THE SEVENTEEN REFERENCES USED FOR GLOSSARY ANALYSIS

The following annotations are made to supplement information presented in the literature review of Chapter II and to present more detailed descriptions of the 17 works listed in Table 3 and analyzed in Table 4. Because these works constitute in a sense the "data" of this thesis, it was considered appropriate to discuss them more fully, particularly the sections of the books or articles that were focused on in this thesis. For annotations of other works mentioned in the dissertation, the reader is referred to *Understanding Body Movement: An Annotated Bibliography* (1972), written by this author.

Allport, Gordon W., and Vernon, Philip E., *Studies in Expressive Movement* (New York: The Macmillan Company, 1933), 269 pp.
This is a major experimental study of individual styles of expressive movement, of "aspects of movement which are distinctive enough to differentiate one individual from another" (p. vii). Following a valuable examination of the literature on consistency in expressive movement and an 11-page list of terms, they describe their motor experiments using 25 men, ages 18 to 50 years. The subjects participated in three experimental sessions, several weeks apart, and were rated on their manner in normal conversation according to observers and to their own ratings. The tests included mechanical measurement of writing pressure, grip pressure, and muscle tonus; measurement of "ordinary" speed and length of stride while walking, estimation of distance between extended limbs, and the like. They obtained good repeat reliabilities and found consistency in the

performance of the same task by different body parts. No "general motility factor" was found, but three "group factors," or traits representing intercorrelations of diverse measures, were discovered: an "emphasis" factor that included such diverse measures as pressure, underestimation of distance, and verbal "slowness"; an "areal" group factor—e.g., area of total writing, length of stride, and overestimation of angles; and a "centrifugal" factor—e.g., overestimation of distances from body, ratings on speech fluency, and underestimation of weights. Four case presentations illustrate how the movement ratings appeared to be congruent with the subject's personality characteristics. Allport and Vernon argue that the physical measures appear more clearly related to psychological phenomena than to other physical measures and conclude that their study supports the notion that there are "organized psychomotor dispositions or expressive traits" (p. 180).

Birdwhistell, Ray L., *Kinesics and Context* (Philadelphia: University of Pennsylvania Press, 1970), 338 pp.

This is a compilation of Birdwhistell's lectures and articles, representing some 20 years of work. It is organized by an editor according to specific topics, so the sources are out of chronological sequence and one is not sure how Birdwhistell himself would develop his exposition. It is a difficult work to summarize because it covers such a wide range of subjects, from mother-infant interaction to differences in body motion of two Kentucky subcultures, and the specific examples of kinesic analysis are often too limited or circumscribed to illustrate the breadth of Birdwhistell's theoretical writing. Most of the examples he cites (such as were examined in this dissertation) deal with a "micro" level of detail—e.g., speech and motion variations over a few seconds. Birdwhistell attends to a great many aspects of movement, particularly to minute details of body part articulation and direction, synchrony between movers, patterns of self-touch, and specific actions such as "eye blinks," head nods, and leg crossing. He considers motion as one channel of the communication system and is concerned with determining the units having communicational significance within a culture. Thus, for him a head movement of two nods may serve a different function in the interaction or have a different communicational significance than one with four nods, and so would constitute a separate kinesic unit.

Although Birdwhistell presents a number of highly detailed examples and an appendix showing his annotation system for describing a wide range of details, the major part of this writing is theoretical; he is laying the groundwork for the still new discipline of kinesics. There are sections on the cultural, learned nature of kinesic patterns and their development in childhood, the place of kinesics in communication and the nature of communication itself, parallels between kinesic and linguistic organization and structures. Also discussed are the vicissitudes of film research and methods for systematically abstracting kinesic units without resorting to controlled experimentation. The essential point is Birdwhistell's rigorous assertion of the role of motion in the cultural communication systems as opposed to a focus on its potential for reflecting inner states and individual or idiosyncratic characteristics.

Condon, W. S., "Linguistic-Kinesic Research and Dance Therapy," *American Dance Therapy Association Proceedings,* Third Annual Conference, 1968, pp. 21-44.

Condon begins with a discussion of the rhythmic, ordered nature of behavior, "rhythmic configurations-of-change," perceptible at various levels, and the problems involved in segmenting or defining units in what is a continuous process. He describes how regularities are discerned after repeated viewing of a film fragment and reports on his principal observations: (a) that an individual's movements are synchronous with each other and with his speech (called personal or self-synchrony), and (b) that two or more people can be seen to move synchronously, the body on one synchronous with "the speech/body motion configurations-of-change of the speaker," called "interactional synchrony" (p. 33). Condon presents a number of "micro-transcriptions" of synchrony that in his work are made from film run at 48 frames per second. A typical example shows about 14 rows for body parts with horizontal demarcations for indicating when parts change direction during a 15-frame segment, parallel with minute speech articulations. Condon illustrates how "behavior seems to be composed of a wave-like, sequential flow of these complex configurations-of-change which emerge into wider and wider harmonious configurations" (p. 31). He gives examples of normal interactional synchrony and of the pathological "self-dyssynchrony" observed in patients with certain neurological disorders, schizophrenia, and autism.

In glossary terms, Condon appears here primarily to be dealing with direction; kinesiological terms such as flexion, extension, and rotation; holds; any body part in great detail; a "micro" level of analysis; and, of course, body part synchrony within the individual and between individuals.

Darwin, Charles, *The Expression of the Emotions in Man and Animals* (1872) (Chicago: University of Chicago Press, 1965), 372 pp.

As has been stated in the thesis, Darwin proposes three principles to explain the origins and functions of various animal and human body expressions, paying particular attention to their evolutionary or ontogenetic bases—i.e., viewing these expressions as vestiges of early adaptive actions. He examines expressions and postures of various domesticated animals, showing how birds may inflate their size to intimidate adversaries, dogs may bare their teeth in preparation for fighting, and horses may paw the ground in impatience. He also has a long section on the origins and interpretations of facial expressions in monkeys. However, he devotes most of this work to an analysis of facial expressions in human beings, using observations of infants, mental patients, actors, peoples around the world, etc. Darwin begins with weeping and its function and development in infants. He posits that the contraction of muscles around the eyes protects them during violent expiration, crying, or screaming. Darwin discusses sad facial expressions, their exaggerated appearance in melancholic patients, and their function in controlling crying. Laughter and smiling are particularly difficult to account for in Darwin's scheme, although he extensively discusses when they occur, what muscles are involved, the onset of smiling in infancy, and the universality of smiling in satisfaction and pleasure. He goes on to analyze the occurrence of frowning, pouting, sneering, body expressions of anger, contempt, helplessness, astonishment, and fear. Darwin focuses on the face and facial muscles although he also describes arm actions and preparatory postures as expressive of emotional states.

Deutsch, Felix, "Analysis of Postural Behavior," *Psychoanalytic Quarterly,* Vol. XVI (1947), pp. 195-213.

Following an initial discussion of references to movement behavior in the psychoanalytic literature, Deutsch presents nine case descriptions of patients he had seen in psychoanalysis and whose positions and movements he had recorded while they were on the couch. He summarizes the principal postures, limb positions, and actions of each patient relative to the psychodynamic themes with which he found them associated. This apparently involved noting both which actions accompanied what verbal remarks and which actions over time appeared to occur with certain underlying themes, as interpreted by Deutsch. For example, a male patient having "fantasies of passive relationships with men" sprawled his legs and spread out his arms. At a later time, when he reported a dream of "masculine assertiveness," he "crossed his legs differently, putting the left over the right, and kept his arms rigidly extended" (p. 204).

Efron, David, *Gesture and Environment* (New York: Kings Crown Press, 1941), 184 pp.

This is a fascinating study of the gestural behavior of first-generation Southern Italians and Eastern European Jews in New York and of their second-generation counterparts. Efron begins with a long discussion of the literature on gestures, particularly of German, racist theories which this study is, in part, designed to refute. He then reports his findings. Efron and an artist spent some two years observing, drawing, and otherwise recording the movements of people talking on the streets of Little Italy, on the Lower East Side, in temples and school gatherings, and at resorts in upstate New York. They supplemented live observation with film study. Efron and his artist-colleague had an eye for all sorts of details in movement and they have arranged their data according to movement parameters such as radius, predominant planes, path or form (e.g., sinuous or straight), the way the upper limbs are articulated, unilateral versus bilateral, tempo, touch patterns, and ways of grouping. There are some fascinating movement phrases accompanying certain words, and comparisons of what Efron calls "ideographic" versus "physiographic" gestures (i.e., traces the thought pattern versus visually depicting an object or spatial relationship or a bodily action) (p. 70). After separately describing the movement characteristics of Eastern Jews and Southern Italians he compares them in an elaborate table. One sees striking differences. Ghetto Jews tend to stand closer together, touch each other a great deal, move the lower arms and hands in a smaller radius in space, describe sinuous paths, and stress ideographic gestures. Ghetto Italians tend to use roundish, bilateral, whole arm gestures in a lateral plane of the physiographic type; they rarely touch each other, and stand more or less apart from each other. The assimilated Jews and Italians tended to lose these dramatic differences and began to resemble each other and the American groups with which they were identifying. Efron includes some interesting descriptions of hybrid gestures in subjects retaining gestural behaviors of two cultures and presents excellent drawings to illustrate his observations.

Ekman, Paul, and Friesen, Wallace V., "Nonverbal Behavior in Psychotherapy Research," in *Research in Psychotherapy,* Vol. III, ed. by J. M. Shlien (Washington, D.C.: American Psychological Association, 1968), pp. 179-216.

The authors extensively discuss the value of studying nonverbal behavior, the kind of information on behavior in general that can be derived from it (particularly in relation to changes in psychological functioning), and problems in defining "units" of nonverbal behavior. They report on a study in which naïve judges observed films of patients at admission and discharge from in-patient psychiatric hospitalization and rated the patients with an adjective check list. Results suggested that nonverbal behavior communicates reliable information to naïve observers and that their judgments are corroborated by other evaluations of the patients.

They go on to a discussion of indicative versus communicative studies of nonverbal behavior—that is, studies that directly measure the behavior and correlate it with other measures to determine its meaning versus studies that involve observer judgments and that examine meaning according to what the movement conveys to others. They then report on a study which involves both modes. Using films of a woman psychiatric patient at admission and discharge, they classified each movement according to its location, duration, and type. Analysis of the "foot acts" at admission and discharge showed marked changes; they became more varied and less repetitious at discharge. Judgments arising from a viewing of foot acts alone showed apparently that the feet communicated unique information. Hand actions were similarly examined. Ekman and Friesen supplement their word descriptions and frequency and duration counts with successive photographs of the gestures taken from the films. They found that actions in the discharge films were different from those at admission and less repetitious. A comparison of the acts themselves with the verbal content themes showed some striking relationships. For example, an action in which hands alternate reaching out into space occurred in the context of a discussion of a conflict involved with taking sides with either her father or her husband (p. 207).

Gesell, Arnold, et al., *The First Five Years of Life* (New York: Harper & Row, 1940), pp. 30, 34-35, 41-42, 46-47, 52-53, 67-107.

The sections of this classic work on early childhood development which were considered in this thesis are the sections on developmental stages in motor coordination, visual-prehensile behavior, posture, and locomotion. The sections on motor development were written primarily by H. M. Halverson, one of the contributing authors, based on direct observation or intensive film analysis of normal children at the Yale Clinic of Child Development. Typically, the children were observed performing basic tasks, walking, climbing stairs, building blocks, playing with a ball, etc., in free nursery play or during structured situations. The normal stages of certain skills are described, often in terms of what the child can do (e.g., can turn pages of a book one at a time), but also in terms of the movement patterns per se. Thus, for example, the authors describe when the infant can hold his head up, sit up, stand, step independently, walk, jump, etc., and also delineate in movement terms some of the patterns involved in development of locomotion such as that at first the child maintains a wide stance, has a low center of gravity, and uses a full-sole step. Attention is paid to balance, dexterity, degree of articulation of body parts, aim and directionality, types of grasp, and patterns of bilaterality, unilaterality, and handedness. Preferences for certain directions at certain ages were tested through observations of children making line drawings. Motor test procedures are described.

Kendon, Adam, "Some Relationships Between Body Motion and Speech: An Analysis of an Example," in *Studies in Dyadic Communication,* ed. by A. W. Seigman and B. Pope (Elmsford, N. Y.: Pergamon Press, 1972), pp. 177-210.

The author conducted a detailed film analysis of the movement and speech of a man in a London pub. This represents one of the first indepth analyses of how movements are organized in relation to the phonetics of relatively long speech units and tonetic stress patterns. The research builds on the observation of Condon that movements of certain "larger" body units may be sustained over larger linguistic units such as phrases, while smaller body parts (e.g., fingers) articulate with smaller segments such as syllables (Kendon, p. 183). Kendon divides speech into "prosodic phrases," which he defines as "the smallest grouping of syllables over which a completed intonation term occurs" (p. 184), and "locutions," which are combinations of phrases roughly corresponding to complete sentences.

He finds there is a distinct shift in posture from the "listening" to the "speaking" intervals and particular trunk and leg movements between "clusters" and locutions. Moreover, each cluster is accompanied by a different arm gesture: right, left, or both. Different head positions "set off" different locutions and each locution is characterized by a different movement, either in terms of direction or in terms of which part is moving. During the smallest unit defined here, the prosodic phrase, there is a distinct direction or "movement to a position." Moreover, Kendon found that specific directions underlined specific words in a logical way; for example, a movement out to an American listener when the Britisher said, "your own race," a movement toward himself with "our own," and a hand thrust outwards with words such as "this" or "that" (p. 203).

In discussing the ramifications of this analysis, Kendon suggests that it is possible that motions accompanying speech partially function as part of the "working memory" for how the speech is to be organized and executed. He states that the intricate relationships between speech and motion he finds suggest that they are "under the guidance of the same controlling mechanism" (p. 206).

Kestenberg, Judith S.; Marcus, Hershey; Robbins, Esther; Berlowe, Jay; and Buelte, Arhnilt, "Development of the Young Child as Expressed Through Bodily Movement I," *Journal of the American Psychoanalytic Association,* Vol. XIX (1972), pp. 746-764.

This is an overview of the stages of movement development from early infancy to age three which integrates psychoanalytic concepts such as psychosexual stages, drive discharge, and development of object relations with detailed observation of infant's movement utilizing Laban's effort-shape analysis. It is something of a synopsis of Kestenberg's principal observations and thinking over 15 years of research on children's movement patterns.

The authors present a schema of the developmental stages in which particular planes of space, shape flow (growing and shrinking patterns) and "tension flow" rhythms (variations in "free" and "bound" movement) are predominant. They maintain that specific rhythms of tension flow serve "phase-specific drive discharge," while shape flow rhythms serve "phase-specific objects." The neonate phase in which infant and mother develop consonant rhythms to facilitate the infant's integration and symbiosis with the mother is described in terms of "growing and shrinking" movements together and adjustments of tension flow. The oral phase is characterized by "oral rhythms" ("smooth transitions from free to bound flow"), exploration of the horizontal plane, and control over widening and narrowing movements. For each stage the authors discuss the role of the predominant movement patterns in relation to body image and ego development and suggest parallels with certain developmental stages of cognition. For example, exploration in the horizontal plane, variations from small enclosed areas to large expanses, and shift from focused attention to a wandering focus are paralleled by the development of object constancy in space.

This paper covers oral, anal, and urethral phases with subsequent phases presumably to be described in a later paper. For each phase, movement patterns in terms of tension and shape flow rhythms, planes stressed, and control over certain spatial dimensions are paralleled with body image, ego organization patterns, and cognitive developments. The anal phase is characterized by smooth, low tension patterns or straining, lengthening, and shortening of the body, development of uprightness, and control over the up-down directions, all paralleled by weight constancy concepts and a growing super-ego. The urethral phase is characterized by "fluid, running" tension flow rhythms, control over the forward-backward dimension, and starting and stopping, which are paralleled by the development of time-constancy concepts and the ability to anticipate and carry out decisions and operations.

Krout, Maurice H., "An Experimental Attempt to Produce Unconscious Manual Symbolic Movements," *Journal of General Psychology,* Vol. LI (1954), pp. 93-120.

Krout delimits his study to "autistic gestures," which he considers self-directed, adaptive reactions to ongoing stimulation which "drain off" impulses but do not affect responses in others. Practically speaking, he focuses on various fidgeting behaviors, patterns of self-touch, and ways of holding one's own hands, which he enumerates and illustrates with drawings. He reports a series of experiments designed to elicit these actions in a controlled way for observation and correlation with specific conflicting statements. That is, subjects were presented with a conflicting statement and asked to reply at once, then presented with a conflicting statement which he was not to reply to until given the nod by the experimenter (actually the experimenter signalled him to reply as soon as the subject had made an autistic gesture). Each of the approximately 100 subjects heard 15 pairs of conflicting statements. Later the subjects were asked to indicate which of 73 attitudes on a list best approximated what he felt during the test series. Information on the procedures, subjects and observers, and specific experimental items is presented. A subsequent article by Krout in the same journal presents the results.

Lomax, Alan; Bartenieff, Irmgard; and Paulay, Forrestine, "Dance Style and Culture" and "The Choreometric Coding Book," in *Folk Song Style and Culture,* ed. by A. Lomax, AAAS Publication No. 88, 1968, pp. 222-247, 262-273.

The authors report preliminary correlations found between movement characteristics of eight large world regions and their socioeconomic subsistence levels (e.g., hunter-gatherers vs. farmers with animal husbandry). This research, called "choreometrics," grew out of an extensive study of folk song styles and cultural differences. Evidence from the analysis of 200 anthropological films suggests that there are movement style areas that cut across national and linguistic boundaries and that these movement styles vary in complexity according to the culture's "subsistence activity." In this framework dance is considered "an adumbration of or derived communication about life, focused on those favored dynamic patterns which most successfully and frequently animated the everyday activity of most of the people in a culture" (p. 223).

They found that body attitude is a major cultural discriminator, that the distinction between the trunk used as two units (as in twisting) and its use as a single unit distinguishes Africa and parts of Maritime Pacific culture from the rest of the world, and that the type of spatial transition from simple reversal to three-dimensional loops correlates with cultural and productive complexity, as does the number of body parts used and the degree of effort and shape complexity.

The authors present a sample of their coding sheets together with definitions and criteria for rating each movement characteristic. In this research they rate the dominant movement patterns of a scene in terms of the most active body parts, body attitude characteristics, spatial transitions, degree of variation in shape and effort qualities, and various body part features such as simultaneous, successive, distal, and "central impulse."

Lowen, Alexander, *Physical Dynamics of Character Structure* (New York: Grune and Stratton, 1958); reprinted as *The Language of the Body* (New York: The Macmillan Company, 1971), 400 pp.

Lowen originally worked with Reich and this book represents his own exploration of personality and character type in relation to posture, muscle tension patterns, and "chronic" bodily expressions. He integrates earlier character analytic concepts and psychoanalytic theory with developing theories of ego psychology. Following a discussion of historical trends up to and including Reich's work and a chapter on the somatic aspects of ego psychology, he reexamines the pleasure principle and the reality principle in relation to physical movement and muscle tension. He presents principles of a "bioenergetic" therapy which represent a combination of psychoanalysis and assessment and direct treatment of the patient's physical habits and movements, arguing that "a therapy which encourages expressive movement increases the motility of the organism, improves its aggression and creates a feeling of strength on both the physical and psychic levels." (p. 115). He devotes chapters to what he calls the oral, masochistic, hysterical, phallic-narcisstic, passive-feminine, schizophrenic, and schizoid characters, using case examples and extensive descriptions of the musculature and postural characteristics of each.

In glossary terms Lowen appears to focus on characteristic postures analyzed according to alignment, configurations of tension or flaccidity, fixed and frozen expressions, weight placement, and strength. He also attends to tensions in any part of the body in a fairly general way, to breathing patterns, and to the individual's tendencies to hold his energy inward or discharge it outward. The focus is on various forms of motor disturbance such as marked hyper- or hypotension, rigidity, and lack of integration.

Mahl, George F., "Gestures and Body Movements in Interviews," in *Research in Psychotherapy,* Vol. III, ed. by J. M. Shlien (1968), pp. 295-346.

Mahl begins by pointing out how neglected the study of body movement in psychotherapy is, and proposes to examine individual differences and intraindividual variations in relation to personality variables through a study of initial psychiatric interviews. The author watched, but could not hear, different patients from behind a one-way mirror and dictated an account of their nonverbal behavior along with immediate clinical impressions. He made inferences about diagnosis, personality traits, areas of conflict, etc., which were subsequently correlated with the verbal content of the session and clinical case records. He noted marked individual sex differences in terms of positions and actions performed. For example, the incidence of pointing was higher in men while "folds arms across waist" was characteristic of women.

Mahl presents an extensive table consisting of three columns: the first a summary of characteristic actions and positions, the second his clinical interpretations, and the third corroborative data from clinical records. For example, the observation "appears very relaxed through-out interview" elicited a prediction from him of "low anxiety" which was substantiated by the interviewer's impression of the patient's "belle indifference" (p. 307). Up to five such correlations are presented for each of thirteen patients, showing rather consistent if somewhat loose corroboration of the nonverbal predictions. Mahl discusses how some gestures may underline, anticipate, or contradict verbal transactions, while others are a direct function of the interaction. He proposes a paradigm for the relationships between the verbalizations and the movements that anticipate them, presenting other clinical examples to support it. Mahl also reports a study of the frequency of various gestures when communicants sit back to back, a topic which was not considered in this dissertation.

North, Marion, *Personality Assessment Through Movement* (London: Macdonald & Evans, 1971), 300 pp.

North's book represents one of the first major attempts to validate certain theories first proposed by Rudolf Laban about the relationships between individual movement dynamics and personality. The author worked extensively with Laban, particularly while he was crystalizing his "effort" analysis and principles for interpreting various patterns of intensity, spatial stress, effort flow, and body coordinations. The first part of the book includes a discussion of movement as expressions and the movement parameters to be considered. Examples of notated effort phrases, and theories for interpreting partial combinations of effort qualities are presented. There are chapters on movement assessment of deaf children, on movement analysis for aptitude assessments, and a section on psychotherapeutic uses of movement. However, the major part of the book deals with a study of 12 school children. Effort assessments of their movement styles were made during a semistructured movement class. These assessments were then compared with teacher evaluations, responses on the Children's Appercception tests, IQ tests, and a "Child Scale B" test for maladjustment from Maudsley Hospital.

Teachers identified the children accurately from the movement assessments alone and the author presents considerable clinical corroboration of her predictions. The movement assessment involved observations of the characteristic planes and directions the child moved in, his predominant effort patterns, balance, dexterity, symmetry, phrase characteristics such as length and rhythm, areas of space used, and inward-outward stress. From these assessments the author interpreted psychological processes such as adaptability, drive, alertness, reasoning ability, creativity, attention, attitudes toward authority, and emotional makeup. Details of the movement assessments of each child are presented along with teacher and test evaluations. This and a lengthy appendix on effort theory make it possible to examine how various movement patterns are psychologically interpreted in North's framework.

Reich, Wilhelm, *Character-Analysis* (New York: Farrar, Straus & Giroux, 1949), 516 pp.

This is a classic psychoanalytic work, the first part of which is widely read theory on character formation and the treatment of character neuroses. Reich extends his analysis beyond considerations of the etiology and treatment of specific neurotic symptoms, such as hysterical paralysis, and proposes "a genetic-dynamic theory of character, a strict differentiation of the contents and the form of the resistances; and, finally, a clinically well-founded differentiation of character types" (p. xix). It is important to note that while Reich was writing on characterology, he saw this subject within a cultural framework and considered that character structures were influenced by socioeconomic and social forces such as a patriarchal family order and that character formation was "anchored" in the social system (p. xxiv).

In the first part of this book Reich presents case material illustrating his theories of character formation and the stages in analyzing resistances. A central theme here is the importance of timing, that the analyst must attend to the manifest behavior and the forms that the patient's resistances take before making interpretations of early infantile conflicts. This explains his great attention to expressive style—to *how* the patient walks, talks, and gestures, as well as to *what* he says and does. As stated in Chapter II of this thesis, Reich takes overt behavior and movement very seriously. In the later parts of *Character-Analysis* he develops theories of the role of muscle "armor," expressive style, the quality of one's movements, and the degrees of mobility in psychological defenses. One finds descriptions of movement patterns typical of various character types threaded through his character analyses. Most relevant to this dissertation are the sections on the relations between muscle armor, binding of anxiety, and "inhibition of every kind of excitation . . ." (p. 347). He argues that there is a segmental arrangement of muscle armor with specific localized tensions reflecting defences against the affects and drives directly expressed by those areas—e.g., inhibition of the pelvis is associated with sexual repression.

Scheflen, Albert E., *The Stream and Structure of Communicational Behavior: Context Analysis of a Psychotherapy Session,* Behavioral Studies Monograph No. 1, Eastern Pennsylvania Psychiatric Institute, 1965, 159 pp.

This is a report of a film analysis of a family therapy session involving Drs. Carl Whitaker and Thomas Malone and a widow and her schizophrenic, 17-year-old daughter. The film of the first session of treatment was analyzed over a number of years using what Scheflen calls a context analysis method. This method involves observation of all behaviors over and over again, tentative selection of those behaviors that occur together, contrast with other such tentative units to determine which elements do or do not occur together, and examination of the context in which the unit occurs. Tentative units are then reexamined to determine if they consistently cluster in certain ways to form units at the next higher level, and so on. Scheflen is countering research in which the experimenter abstracts and measures behaviors out of context or imputes psychological meaning out of his own judgment and experience.

The monograph has sections on Scheflen's communication systems orientation and on the rules, regulations, and organization of face-to-face group behaviors. He describes the individuals involved and their individual performances, but the bulk of the work deals with the patterns of group behavior as they are hierarchically ordered. For example, two distinct "periods" of behaviors that are demarcated by postural shifts by the daughter were isolated. Considered together, the periods combined into distinct "cycles," and the cycles combined into an overall phase. Scheflen perceives a phenomenal regularity. The pipe cleaning ritual and "lag step progression" of actions and postural shifts of the two therapists is particularly "program-like," so much so that if one omitted a step, the other fidgeted until the first came around (p. 118). Scheflen cites a number of special observations, such as "regulatory signals" which affect the speed of progress, and he defines three communication units: the "point," which is characterized by a head and eye shift and hold; the "position," which is a combination of one or more points "junctured" by major postural shifts; and the "presentation," which is the "natural program of positions taken by an interactant for the duration" of the time that he is present in one place (p. 63). It is difficult to summarize Scheflen's intricate analysis. He approaches the session from a number of angles: the individual performances, the interrelationships and complementarities of behaviors, the regular oscillations of behaviors, role shifts, and the specific "points" and "positions" as determined through his context analysis. He discusses the ramifications of this analysis of "psychotherapy as a programmed interaction," using this specific example of a family therapy session to discuss fundamental problems in group research.

APPENDIX II

*Selected References on Movement Notation
Systems and Their Application*

SELECTED REFERENCES ON MOVEMENT NOTATION SYSTEMS AND THEIR APPLICATION

The following annotated references are presented as a supplement to Chapter III for researchers interested in investigating this area further. In this country, the major "clearinghouse" for literature on dance and movement notations is the Dance Notation Bureau (19 Union Square W., New York City); most of the references below can be bought or read there. The Dance Notation Bureau also provides extensive training in Labanotation and Effort-shape Analysis. Notation experts for consultation may be contacted through the Bureau.

A. Labanotation

1. Hutchinson, Ann, *Labanotation* (rev. and expanded ed.; New York: Theater Arts Books, 1970), 528 pp.

This is the most extensive and elaborate text on movement notation for any of the systems. An enormous range of concepts and detailed analyses are discussed and illustrated with drawings and notations. A very useful book for anyone interested in how specific problems in movement analysis can be tackled.

2. Laban, Rudolf, *Principles of Dance and Movement Notation* (London: Macdonald and Evans, Ltd., 1956), 56 pp.

A good introduction to Laban's approach and his "thinking."

3. Laban, Rudolf, *The Mastery of Movement*, ed. by L. Ullmann (2nd ed., rev.; London: Macdonald and Evans, Ltd., 1960), 186 pp.

Of particular interest here for its sections on psychological interpretation of movement and cultural patterns in movement.

4. Goodman, Nelson, *Languages of Art* (Indianapolis: The Bobbs-Merrill Co., 1968), 277 pp.

An important examination of "symbol systems" and processes of devising, applying, and interpreting them. Includes a consideration of Labanotation and how it "meets the requirements for a notational language" (p. 214).

5. Preston-Dunlap, Valerie, "A Notation System for Recording Observable Motion," *International Journal of Man-Machine Studies,* Vol. I (1969), pp. 361-386.

This is valuable as an introduction to how Labanotation, an abbreviated form of it called "motif writing," and two forms of "effort" recording may be applied to analysis of functional activity. It is a rare example of how approaches can be combined to analyze the same movement.

B. Effort-shape Analysis

1. Dell, Cecily, *A Primer for Movement Description: Using Effort-shape and Supplementary Concepts* (New York: Dance Notation Bureau Publication, 1970), 123 pp.

The best presentation of this system, it has numerous behavioral examples and an appendix on how to analyze and record phrases of movement with effort-shape notation.

2. Bartenieff, Irmgard, and Davis, Martha, "Effort-shape Analysis of Movement: The Unity of Expression and Function," Albert Einstein College of Medicine, Bronx, New York, 1965, 71 pp. (Unpublished monograph.)

An initial exposition of effort-shape analysis of movement with examples of how it may be used in developmental, personality and group interaction research.

3. Laban, Rudolf, and Lawrence, F. C., *Effort* (London: Macdonald and Evans, Ltd., 1947), 88 pp.

An initial presentation of Laban's "Effort" analysis and theories of the interpretation of "effort dynamics."

4. Bartenieff, Irmgard; Davis, Martha; and Paulay, Forrestine, *Four Adaptations of Effort Theory in Research and Teaching* (New York: Dance Notation Bureau Publications, 1972).

Notable here for the chapter on the logic of effort-shape analysis and its systematic use in research and for the chapter on its application to the cross-cultural study of dance.

5. Bartenieff, Irmgard, and Davis, Martha, "An Analysis of the Movement Behavior Within a Group Psychotherapy Session," presented at the Conference of the American Group Psychotherapy Association, Chicago, 1968.

An application of "effort analysis" to the assessment of the movement styles of various members and movement patterns in the group.

6. Davis, Martha, "An Effort-shape Movement Analysis of a Family Therapy Session," Yeshiva University, 1966, 21 pp. (Unpublished paper.)

This work presents specific notated examples of speech and movement correlations that were found in the group. It also demonstrates how movement dynamics may vary dramatically with various symptoms.

7. North, Marion, *Personality Assessment Through Movement* (London: Macdonald and Evans, Ltd., 1971), 300 pp.

The most elaborate application of effort analysis to individual movement style; it has sections on theories of interpretation of the effort variables.

8. Kestenberg, Judith S., "The Role of Movement Patterns in Development: II—Flow of Tension and Effort," *Psychoanalytic Quarterly,* Vol. XXXIV (1965), pp. 517-563.

Adapting Laban's effort theory and particular concepts of "effort flow" and "effort" elements to psychoanalytic assessments of early motor patterns reflecting "drive discharge."

9. Kestenberg, Judith S., "The Role of Movement Patterns in Development: III—The Control of Shape," *Psychoanalytic Quarterly,* Vol. XXXVI (1967), pp. 356-409.

Utilizing Laban's concepts of "shape flow" and "shaping," the author examines relationships between the development of various planes and spatial characteristics in the child's movement and various psychosexual stages.

C. Eshkol-Wachmann Movement Notation

1. Eshkol, Noa, and Wachmann, Abraham, *Movement Notation* (London: Weidenfeld and Nicholson, 1958), 203 pp.

A meticulously prepared and illustrated textbook which has numerous examples of notated movements. Generally, the examples are total body movements such as occur in dance. The reader is referred to the references below, which illustrate how the Eshkol-Wachmann system may be adapted for behavioral study.

2. Eshkol, Noa, *The Hand Book* (Tel Aviv: The Movement Notation Society, 1971), 135 pp.

Following a brief summary of the principles of Eshkol-Wachmann notation, the author presents extensive illustrations and notations of hand and upper body movements of deaf sign language and the "mudras" hand forms of Indian classical dance.

3. Golani, Ilan, and Zeidel, Shmuel, *The Golden Jackal* (Tel Aviv: The Movement Notation Society, 1969), 124 pp.

From this one can get an idea of how Eshkol-Wachmann notation may be used in a study of the behavior of a pair of animals, in this case, jackals.

4. Eshkol, N.; Melvin, P.; Michl, J.; Von Foerster, H., and Wachmann, A., *Notation of Movement* (Urbana: Biological Computer Laboratory, University of Illinois, 1970), 163 pp.

This is a report on the collaboration of Eshkol-Wachmann specialists, computer scientists, and physical educators whose goal was to transcribe the notation into a computer program and evolve a "unified system of descriptions, commands and execution of movements, may they be performed by a human body, by artificial limbs or automata, or by computer simulations" (p. i). After an introduction to Eshkol-Wachmann notation, the notational computer programs and their development are presented.

D. Additional Notation Literature

1. Hutchinson, Ann, "Survey and Comparison of Dance Notation Through the Ages: Parts I and II," 1972. (Unpublished.)

This is a scholarly analysis and comparison of early forms of letter and stick-figure recordings as well as systems such as Eshkol-Wachmann and Labanotation.

2. Benesh, Rudolph, and Benesh, Joan, *An Introduction to Benesh Dance Notation* (London: A. & C. Black, 1956), 48 pp.

This is a popular notation system which is particularly good for recording the path of the movement.

3. Canna, D. J., and Loring, Eugene, *Kineseography: The Loring System of Dance Notation* (N.p.: Academy Press, 1955), 57 pp.

This system utilizes arrows for directions, symbols for body postures, and distinguishes between "extroverted" and "introverted" characteristics of movement.

4. Morris, Margaret, *The Notation of Movement* (London: Kegan Paul, Trench, Trubner and Co., 1928), 103 pp.

Includes symbols for direction, flexion-extension, rotation, and pronation-supination, and is notable for its attention to ways of recording breathing and facial movements.

BODY MOVEMENT
Perspectives in Research
An Arno Press Collection

Anthropological Perspectives of Movement
  a. LaBarre, Weston
     The Cultural Basis of Emotions and Gestures (Reprinted from *Journal of Personality,* Vol. 16, 1947)
  b. Bailey, Flora L.
     Navaho Motor Habits (Reprinted from *American Anthropologist,* Vol. 44, 1942)
  c. Hewes, Gordon W.
     World Distribution of Certain Postural Habits (Reprinted from *American Anthropologist,* Vol. 57, 1955)
  d. Kurath, Gertrude Prokosch
     Panorama of Dance Ethnology (Reprinted from *Current Anthropology,* Vol. 1, May 1960)
  e. Hall, Edward T.
     A System for the Notation of Proxemic Behavior (Reprinted from *American Anthropologist,* Vol. 65, 1963)
  f. Hayes, Francis
     Gestures: A Working Bibliography (Reprinted from *Southern Folklore Quarterly,* Vol. 21, 1957)

Christiansen, Bjørn
Thus Speaks the Body: Attempts Toward a Personology from the Point of View of Respiration and Postures. Oslo, Norway, 1963

Davis, Martha
Towards Understanding the Intrinsic in Body Movement. New York, 1974

Dewey, Evelyn
Behavior Development in Infants: A Survey of the Literature on Prenatal and Postnatal Activity 1920–1934. New York, 1935

Evolution of Facial Expression: Two Accounts
   a. Andrew, R. J.
      The Origin and Evolution of the Calls and Facial Expressions of the Primates (Reprinted from *Behaviour,* Vol. 20, Leiden, Netherlands, 1963)
   b. Huber, Ernst
      Evolution of Facial Musculature and Facial Expression. Baltimore, 1931

Facial Expression in Children: Three Studies
   a. Washburn, Ruth Wendell
      A Study of the Smiling and Laughing of Infants in the First Year of Life (Reprinted from *Genetic Psychology Monographs,* Vol. 6, Nos. 5 & 6, Worcester, Mass., 1929) November–December, 1929
   b. Spitz, René A., with the Assistance of K. M. Wolf
      The Smiling Response: A Contribution to the Ontogenesis of Social Relations (Reprinted from *Genetic Psychology Monographs,* Vol. 34, Provincetown, Mass., 1946) August, 1946
   c. Goodenough, Florence L.
      Expression of the Emotions in a Blind-Deaf Child (Reprinted from *Journal of Abnormal and Social Psychology,* Vol. 27, Lancaster, Pa., 1932)

Psychoanalytic Perspectives of Movement
   a. Ferenczi, S.
      Psycho-analytical Observations on Tic (Reprinted from *The International Journal of Psycho-Analysis,* Vol. 2, March, 1921)
   b. Feldman, Sandor
      The Blessing of the Kohenites (Reprinted from *American Imago,* Vol. 2, 1941)
   c. Kris, Ernst
      Laughter as an Expressive Process: Contributions to the Psycho-Analysis of Expressive Behaviour (Reprinted from *International Journal of Psycho-Analysis,* Vol. 21, 1940)
   d. Mahler, Margaret Schoenberger
      Tics and Impulsions in Children: A Study of Motility (Reprinted from *Psycho-Analytic Quarterly,* Vol. 5, 1944)
   e. Deutsch, Felix
      Analytic Posturology (Reprinted from *Psycho-Analytic Quarterly,* Vol. 21, 1952)
   f. Braatoy, Trygve
      Psychology vs. Anatomy in the Treatment of "Arm Neuroses"

with Physiotherapy (Reprinted from *Journal of Nervous and Mental Disease,* Vol. 115, 1952)
- g. Mittelmann, Bela
  Psychodynamics of Motility (Reprinted from *Psychoanalytic Study of the Child,* Vol. 39, 1958)
- h. Kestenberg, Judith S.
  Rhythm and Organization in Obsessive-Compulsive Development (Reprinted from *The International Journal of Psycho-Analysis,* Vol. 47, 1966)

Recognition of Facial Expression
- a. Jenness, Arthur
  The Recognition of Facial Expressions of Emotion (Reprinted from *Psychological Bulletin,* Vol. 29, 1932)
- b. Frois-Wittmann, J.
  The Judgment of Facial Expression (Reprinted from *Journal of Experimental Psychology,* Vol. 13, 1930)
- c. Landis, Carney
  The Interpretation of Facial Expression In Emotion (Reprinted from *Journal of General Psychology,* Vol. 2, 1929)
- d. Frijda, Nico H.
  The Understanding of Facial Expression of Emotion (Reprinted from *Acta Psychologica,* Vol. 9, 1953)
- e. Schlosberg, Harold
  Three Dimensions of Emotion (Reprinted from *Psychological Review,* Vol. 61, March 1954)
- f. Honkavaara, Sylvia
  The Psychology of Expression (Reprinted from *British Journal of Psychology:* Monograph Supplements No. 32, 1961)

Research Approaches to Movement and Personality
- a. Eisenberg, Philip
  Expressive Movements Related to Feeling of Dominance (Reprinted from *Archives of Psychology,* Vol. 30, No. 211, New York, 1937) May, 1937
- b. Bartenieff, Irmgard and Martha Davis
  Effort-Shape Analysis of Movement: The Unity of Expression and Function. New York, 1965
- c. Takala, Martti
  Studies of Psychomotor Personality Tests I. Helsinki, Finland, 1953

Wolff, Charlotte
A Psychology of Gesture. Translated from the French Manuscript by Anne Tennant. 2nd edition. London, 1948